Rict Walker

# THE COUNTRY DIVINE

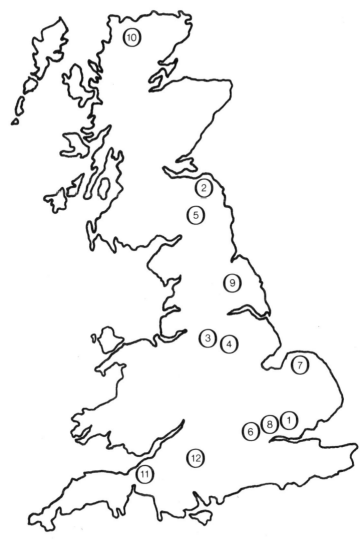

1. Earls Colne
2. Tyninghame
3. Stodhart
4. Treswell
5. Stitchill
6. Landbeach

7. Weston Longville
8. Broxbourne
9. Wath
10. Strath Naver
11. Camerton
12. Langley Burrel

# THE COUNTRY DIVINE

## Michael Brander

THE SAINT ANDREW PRESS
EDINBURGH

First published in 1981 by
*THE SAINT ANDREW PRESS*
121 George Street, Edinburgh EH2 4YN

Copyright © Michael Brander 1981

ISBN 0 7152 0492 0

*Printed and bound in Hong Kong by Wing King Tong Co Ltd*

To
# The Five Shots from the Canon
Margaret, Mary, Dorothea, Jean, Serena

# Contents

Frontispiece iii
List of Illustrations x
Preface xi
Introduction 1

1 The Rev. Ralph Josselin
Puritan Farmer and Businessman: Essex 17

2 The Rev. George Turnbull
Early Presbyterian Minister: East Lothian 31

3 The Rev. James Clegg
Peak District Minister and Physician: Derbyshire 47

4 The Rev. Seth Ellis Stevenson
Schoolmaster and Pluralist: Nottinghamshire 63

5 The Rev. George Ridpath
Border Minister and Historian: Roxburghshire 73

6 The Rev. William Cole
Philosopher and Antiquarian: Buckinghamshire 89

7 The Rev. James Woodforde
Farmer and Gourmand: Somerset and Norfolk 107

8 The Rev. William Jones
Henpecked Curate and Vicar: Hertfordshire 123

9 The Rev. Bejamin Newton
Squarson of Wath: Yorkshire 139

10 The Three Sages: Aeneas, Alexander and Donald
Highland Ministers: Sutherland 155

11 The Rev. John Skinner
Neurotic Antiquarian: Somerset 171

12 The Rev. Francis Kilvert
Victorian Curate: Welsh Borders 187

Select Bibliography 212
Further Reading 213

# Illustrations

The road to Colchester framing the church tower at
Earls Colne in Essex.    16

A view of the Bass Rock and the East Lothian coastline
from Tyninghame.    30

The Presbyterian church at Stodhart, near Chapel-
en-le-Frith in the Peak District.    46

The church at Treswell, near Retford.    62

A pastoral view of the Eildon Hills from the east of the
kirk and manse at Stitchill.    72

Landbeach, alongside the village pound.    88

The late fifteenth-century beautifully preserved rood
screen at Weston Longville.    106

The church at Broxbourne and the vicarage alongside.    122

A distant view of the church at Wath.    138

A sheep grazing in the ruins of the township of
Grumbeg, above Loch Naver.    154

The church in the Somerset valley below Camerton,
close to Bath.    170

The church at Langley Burrell, close to Chippenham,
in Wiltshire.    186

# Preface

It was the late Bryen Gentry, erstwhile Managing Director of Cassells and founder of Gentry Books, a man of very great experience in publishing, who originally suggested that there was an interesting and largely unexplored field of literature to be found in the diaries of the country divines. This book is the result. Covering the years from 1616 to 1880 it is primarily a book about people. It is a study, largely in their own words, of varying personalities over those centuries, in parts of Britain as far apart as Sutherland and Somerset, whose only common factor was that they were country pastors of one denomination or another who kept diaries of their daily lives. As far as possible they have been allowed to portray their own individual characteristics, their own strengths and weaknesses, revealing their own way of life. Where it has been necessary to set the scene, the time and the place, this has also been done, as far as possible, in their own words. A common religion and a country background form a link between them over the centuries.

Priest, pastor, minister, preacher, high church or low church, a common pattern of humanity emerges. Workers, idlers, intellectuals, sportsmen, ascetics, psychologists, psychopaths, all are to be found among clerics as among laymen. To a greater or a lesser degree their religious duties were carried out faithfully enough. It is primarily their personal life and their characters which are presented in their own words. From these self-portraits, the country divine's changing place in society may be traced over the centuries, influenced throughout, inevitably, by the powerful conflicting political forces of religion and the land.

Being mainly educated men, frequently with time on their hands, the country divines left an increasingly well-documented account of their activities from the seventeenth century onwards, as the clerical diaries and other works listed in the bibliography bear witness, although these are by no means exhaustive. Many of them, as may well be imagined, are as dull as mouthed and muttered sermons, or dry as long forgotten sectarian disputes. Others vividly portray the personality of the cleric, revealing his thoughts and attitudes, as well as casting an interesting sidelight on the life of the countryside at the time.

The aim has been to include only the latter type of diaries, some well known and some obscure, while covering as wide a cross-section of Britain as possible and at the same time providing a series of nearly consecutive self-portraits over the centuries. Due simply to lack of space much has had to be left out, not least from the diaries themselves. Such well-known names as Gilbert White, Sydney Smith, Hawker of Morwenstow and Baring Gould, or lesser-known characters such as Henry Justinian Newcome, to mention only a few, have been reluctantly excluded for this reason. There have unfortunately had to be vast omissions and for these and for any errors of commission I apologise to the reader.

For the photographs, my thanks are due to Patrick Douglas-Hamilton, who travelled with me upwards of 2,000 miles around the U.K. to take them especially for this book.

My thanks for their invaluable help are due also to many people, but particularly for reading the manuscript and commenting on it I would like to thank Mr K.H. Grose, Mr J.R. Clark, the Rev. Kenneth Hughes and the Rev. Bernard B. Humphreys. Their helpful comments were of inestimable value but they can in no way be held responsible for any errors of omission or commission, which are entirely mine. For their assistance in providing volumes listed in the bibliography, or their courtesy in providing facilities for reading manuscripts my thanks must go to the Librarian and staff of the National Library of Scotland; Miss Christine Wright and staff of the National Lending Library Inter-Library-Loans Service and the many Librarians throughout

Scotland and the UK thus involved in providing books for research. My thanks are due also to the Librarian and staff of the Edinburgh Public Library; Mr Brian M. Gall, the Librarian and staff of the East Lothian County Council Library and the Haddington Library; Mr Gil Swift, Director of Leisure of the Metropolitan Borough of Wigan; Mr G.A. Knight, Archivist of Wigan Record Office; the Librarian and staff of the Bury St. Edmund's Public Library, the Rev. A.S.J. Holden at Earls Colne, and many others.

Finally my thanks must also go to my wife Evelyn and my daughter Kathleen for help in the endless task of proof-reading.

# Introduction

The history of the country divine, the village priest and the village church, go back to Saxon times, when the Lord of the Manor frequently built his own church and appointed his own incumbent. His income was obtained from the 'glebe' land gifted with the living, also from offerings by his parishioners and from the 'tithe' or tenth part of the produce of the fields, of the breeding stock and of the labour, which in turn he was expected to use for the good of the poor and needy. Many of these early Saxon divines were almost certainly relatives of the Lord of the Manor and it is significant that as early as the reign of King Edgar (957-975) Archbishop Dunstan was forced to decree that priests should not hunt, hawk or dice, from which it may be inferred that they had been accustomed to taking part in such pursuits. Admittedly he also had to forbid any priest 'to be an ale-scop [i.e. a reciter in an ale-house] nor in any way to act the gleeman'. It would thus seem that there were already clear social divisions in the ranks of the clergy.

After the Conquest the Norman Lord of the Manor frequently gifted the advowson, or right to choose the incumbent, to a monastic house, which all too often appropriated the tithes to its own use and installed an appointee known as *vicarius*, or substitute rector. It was not long before semi-educated peasant priests, known as *capellani*, (i.e. assistant curates) were being appointed as the abuse termed pluralism, or the holding of several livings by one clergyman, became more common. In 1175 Archbishop Richard of Canterbury, Thomas à Becket's successor, may be noted decreeing: 'Let no clerks in Holy Orders go to eat in taverns, nor be present at drinking bouts. . . . Let the offender desist or be deposed.' Yet in spite of such attempts to check abuses the standards of the country priest continued to decline steadily.

In *The Vision of Piers Plowman*, attributed to William Langland (c. 1362), there is a satirical portrait of the parish priest named Sloth, of thirty years' standing and unable to read properly. In Chaucer's *Canterbury Tales* (c. 1388) there is on the other hand the idealised portrait of the 'pure parson' from which, by inference, the more general picture, the mirror image, may be drawn.

> He was a shepherde and noght a mercenarie.
> And thogh he hooly were and vertuous,
> He was to synful men nat despitous,
> Ne of his speche daungerous ne digne,
> But in his techyng discreet and benygne.
> To drawne folk to hevene by fairnesse,
> By good ensample, this was his bisynesse.
> But it were any persone obstinat,
> What so he were, of heigh or lough estat,
> Hym wolde he snybben sharply for the nonys,
> A bettre preest I trowe that nowher noon ys.
> He waited after no pompe and reverence,
> Ne maked him a spiced conscience,
> But Cristes loore and his apostles twelve,
> He taughte, but first he folwed it hymselve.
>                                    (Prologue 514-528)

With the growth of the monastic houses and increasing power of the bishops and superior clergy, the affairs of Church and State gradually became inextricably mixed. It was often next to impossible to disentangle the politics of the State from purely ecclesiastical problems. Thus the death of Thomas à Becket may be viewed as simply one incident in the developing political struggle between Church and State, between the power of the Pope in Rome as spiritual ruler over Christendom and the power of the temporal rulers over their individual kingdoms.

During the fourteenth century there was a strong reaction within the Church itself against this type of worldly Christianity back to a more self-sacrificing, religious way of life. In England this was inspired by the preaching and writings of John Wycliffe, rector of Lutterworth in Leicestershire. It was

Wycliffe's philosophy which inspired John Ball, the itinerant preacher who was among the leaders of the Peasants' Revolt of 1381. The latter's revolutionary concepts were far in advance of his day and he inveighed against social injustice with such texts as:

> When Adam delved and Eve span
> Who was then the gentleman?

Although the Peasants' Revolt was ruthlessly suppressed and John Ball himself was hanged, drawn and quartered, the forces thus set in motion, the so-called Lollards, were not so easily contained. During the fifteenth and sixteenth centuries Lollardism spread throughout England and Scotland despite continual persecution. Meanwhile Wycliffe's philosophy had been carried to Bohemia by scholars in the train of Richard II's queen, Anne of Bohemia, and there it was eagerly taken up by John Huss, who raised it to the level of a national religion. Although condemned and burned for heresy, Huss in turn influenced Luther. By the time the doctrines of Luther and Erasmus had supplanted those of Wycliffe in England, the Reformation was well under way. Despite all the political power struggles between Church and State, the ultimate changes stemmed from the grass roots, from the itinerant preachers such as John Ball, or the philosophers such as John Wycliffe, rector of Lutterworth, and from the broad mass of the people themselves.

It required the absolute power of a Tudor monarch combined with the megalomania of Henry VIII to abolish papal authority at a stroke in 1534 and to follow this up five years later with the dissolution of the monasteries and the introduction of the Six Articles of Religion, but there can be little doubt that a great part of the nation was prepared to accept the changes, even if in many cases anti-clericalism, or apathy, were their prime reasons for doing so. Admittedly, during her short reign from 1553 to 1558, Mary demonstrated that there was still strong support for the old religion with determined backing from the throne, but the flames which consumed Ridley, Latimer and Cranmer, as well as some fifty or more fellow martyrs each year of her reign, merely helped to forge a steel-hard core of Protestantism.

Following the Reformation there was inevitably a lengthy period of deep religious change and upset as the whole approach to Christian worship underwent a radical transformation in England. The old reliance on ritual and symbolism was condemned as superstition and there was much needless destruction of church architecture and ornament. Religious teaching was circumscribed by the English Bible and the Book of Common Prayer. The Puritans and more extreme Protestants moved away from the celebration of Saints' Days and similar festivals, concentrating instead on the importance of the Sabbath as a day of prayer.

When Elizabeth re-established the Protestant Church by the Acts of Supremacy and Uniformity in 1559 soon after coming to the throne, there was little persecution of Roman Catholics and this continued for the next decade of her reign. It was not until her excommunication by Pope Pius in 1570 that harsher measures were instituted. With the Pope sending active support for the rebellion in Ireland and a Jesuit Mission to England, open support for Roman Catholicism came to be regarded not as a question of religious tolerance, but of treachery to the throne. With the rising tide of English nationalism it became a patriotic duty for Englishmen beset by Roman Catholic enemies to embrace Protestantism. The right of choice, whether Roman Catholic or Puritan, was not conceded. Yet despite the fact that by the end of Elizabeth's long reign the majority of Englishmen were ardent Protestants, there were still some faithful to the old religion as well as a growing number of Puritans.

On John Knox's death in 1572 he was succeeded as leader of the church by Andrew Melville, to whom James VI was 'Christ's silly vassal'. Elizabeth warned James against the pretensions of such men 'who have no king but a presbytery', yet it was noticeable that when James was at odds with his ministers she openly, or secretly, backed the kirk. In 1580 Episcopacy was abolished by the Assembly and a clear division was established between the Church of Scotland and the Church of England. For the time Presbyterianism flourished, but it was not long before James was attempting to restore the power of the bishops. The seeds were sown then for the religious dissension which was to grip Scotland throughout the ensuing century.

In all faiths and creeds, then as always, there were high standards set by some. The dedication of the members of the various Jesuit missions sent to England from Rome to minister to the remaining Roman Catholic faithful has to be admired. It must have been an uncomfortable and perilous experience travelling through the country in disguise, slipping from priest's hole to priest's hole, always at the mercy of informers and faced with the unpleasant prospect of incarceration in the Tower, torture and execution should they be caught. Such was the fate of Fathers Campion and Parsons, to name only two of the more notable. Few were as fortunate as Father Gerard, who succeeded in escaping spectacularly from the Tower and returning to the Continent where he ended his days in exile.

There were, no doubt, many saintly-minded Puritan clerics such as the rector of Dry Drayton in Cambridgeshire, Richard Greenham (1570-1590), who believed wholeheartedly in reserving the Sabbath for worship and in ignoring all Saints' Days. Yet during the same period there were also, regrettably, many others like the pluralist rector of Willing Doe and Beauchamp Roding in Essex, who was found guilty of 'beynge a druncarde' and was condemned to present himself 'in the markett of Chelmsforde with a white shete and a white rodde in his hande confessing his fallte'.

Although the Elizabethan settlement brought gradual

order out of chaos, there was a steady divergence of thought and practice during the later sixteenth and early seventeenth centuries between the Puritan and more extreme Protestant on the one hand, and the broader-minded attitude of the majority on the other. The former took as their ideal a plain white-washed church, lengthy sermons and rigid observance of Sunday worship, ignoring the Saints' Days, whereas the latter gradually reverted to such Catholic practices as the wearing of surplices, the presence of candles and a cross on the altar, the chanting of the ritual and observance of feast days. The example set by some leading clerics such as the saintly Bishop of Winchester, Launcelot Andrewes, encouraged these tendencies, as indeed did dislike of the wearisome dogmatism of the more extreme Calvinists.

The views of the extreme Puritans such as the pamphleteering Stubbs brothers, John and Philip, were only calculated to gain the support of those already like-minded. In 1597, for example, John expressed his disgust at the projected marriage of Elizabeth to the Duke of Anjou in an outburst entitled 'The Discoverie of a Gaping Gulf whereinto England is likely to be Swallowed by another French Marriage'. Sentenced to lose his right hand for sedition, he protested his innocence to the last, afterwards raising his hat with his left hand and crying 'God Save the Queen' before fainting away.

It was possible to admire John Stubbs' misguided loyalty and patriotism, but Philip's virulence and bigotry, as displayed in his *Anatomie of Abuses* published in 1583, was another matter. Railing against the celebration of May Day, he wrote: 'Against Maie-day ... all the young men and maides, old men and wives, run gadding overnight to the woods, groves, hills and mountains, where they spend all the night in pleasant pastimes and in the morning they return bringing with them birche boughes and branches of trees to deck their assemblies withal. But their chiefest jewel they bring from thence is the Maie-pole, which they bring home with great veneration, as thus — they have twentie or fourtie yoake of oxen, every oxe having a sweet nosegaie of flowers tied to the tip of his hornes, and these oxen drawe home the May-poale, their stinking idol rather, which they covered all over with flowers and hearbes, bound round with strings from the top to the bottom, and sometimes it was painted with variable colours, having two or three hundred men, women and children following it with great devotion. And thus equipped it was reared with handkerchiefs and flagges streaming on the top, they strawe the ground round about it, they bind green boughs about it, they set up summer halles, bowers and arbours hard by it, and then fall they to banquetting and feasting, to leaping and dauncing about it, as the heathen people did at the dedication of their idolls. I have heard it crediblie reported, by men of great gravity, credite, and reputation, that of fourtie, three-score, or an hundred maides going to the woode, there have scarcely the third part of them returned home againe as they went . . .'

Contemporary with Philip Stubbs, but happily devoid of any such self-defeating bigotry and spleen, was the rector of Bishopsbourne near Canterbury from 1591 to 1600, Richard Hooker, 'judicious' in all but his choice of wife. Although he ended his days as a hen-pecked philosopher, he wrote *The Laws of Ecclesiastical Politie*, which laid down with clarity the foundations of Anglicanism. It was on these that the character of the Church of England was to develop, not on the extremes of Puritanism or of Anglo-Catholicism.

The movement of the Church towards Catholicism and the persecution of the Puritans was accelerated under the aegis of William Laud, Archbishop of Canterbury from 1633 to his execution by direction of the Long Parliament in 1645. Intensely opposed to Calvinism in any form and a strong believer in the importance of ceremony and ritual, by his complete insensitivity to popular opinion and lack of statesmanship, he did as much as the king to provoke the rebellion against the Crown. The Puritan emigration to Massachusetts, which began in 1629 and continued until his impeachment and imprisonment in 1640, was caused largely by his despotic administration. His involvement of the Church in politics and affairs of State was fatal both to himself and to ecclesiastical unity.

Among the more notable country divines under Archbishop Laud were Nicholas Ferrar, deacon of Little Gidding in Huntingdonshire and George Herbert, vicar of Bemerton near Salisbury. It was due largely to his friendship with Ferrar that Herbert, the fifth son of Sir Richard Herbert and brother of Lord Herbert of Cherbury, became vicar of Bemerton in 1630. Poet and courtier, with such vicar friends as Izaac Walton, Bishop Andrewes, Francis Bacon and Dr Donne, Herbert wrote 'a complet pastoral' entitled *A Priest to the Temple: or The Country Parson, his Character and Rule of Holy Life*. This collection of *Sacred Poems and Private Ejaculations* was privately published at Cambridge by Nicholas Ferrar a year after the poet's death.

He wrote that on Sunday the country parson, 'when the hour calls, with his family attending him, he goes to church, at his first entrance humbly adoring and worshipping the invisible majesty and presence of Almighty God, and blessing the people, either openly or to himself. Then having read divine service twice fully, and preached in the morning, and catechised in the afternoon, he thinks he hath in some measure, according to poor and frail man, discharged the public duties of the congregation. The rest of the day he spends either in reconciling neighbours that are at variance, or in visiting the sick, or in exhortations to some of his flock by themselves, whom his sermons cannot, or do not reach. . . . He useth and preferreth ordinary church catechism, partly for obedience to authority, partly for uniformity sake . . .'

Herbert practised what he preached and advised his own

wife: 'You are now a minister's wife, and must now so far forget your father's house as not to claim precedence of any of your parishioners; for you are to know, that a priest's wife can challenge no precedence or place, but that which she purchases by her obliging humility, and I am sure, places so purchased do best become them.'

As Izaac Walton recorded: 'The humble farm labourers working in the fields let their plough rest when Mr. Herbert's saints' bell rung to prayers, that they might offer their devotions to God with him.' Although Herbert devoted his life to a practical example of Christian piety, by following the Laudian style he necessarily accepted the symbols and vestments approved by higher authority and kept all the feasts and festivals according to the Prayer Book. While this form of Christianity appealed to Roman Catholics it was anathema to the Puritans, who apostrophised the clerics adopting it in a biting ballad around 1635 as follows:

> His Divinity is trust up with five points,
> He drops, ducks, bowes, as made all of joints;
> But when his Romane nose stands full East,
> He feares neither God nor beast.

It was as well for him that the pious Herbert died in 1631 and was spared the indignity of being plundered by Parliamentary forces during the Civil Wars, or of being turned out of his living by the Puritans during the Commonwealth, as were many royalist or Laudian clerics throughout the country. One such was the pastoral lyrist, poet of nature and innumerable real or imaginary loves, Robert Herrick, vicar of Deane Prior on the edge of Dartmoor from 1629 to 1647, and again from 1662 to 1674.

Born and bred in London, the poet was educated at Westminster school and then at St. John's College, Cambridge, after being apprenticed to his uncle Sir William Herrick, a notable goldsmith. Robert Herrick was a contemporary and friend of Ben Jonson and other leading poets

and wits of the day. Ordained in 1629 he was presented to
the living of Deane Prior by the king. Although at first he
resented his isolation in the depths of Devon he soon came
to appreciate the delights of his rural solitude, with its Morris
dances, Twelfth night celebrations, wakes and other revels,
which he immortalised in verse. Truly he wrote:

> I sing of brooks, of blossoms, birds and bowers:
> Of April, May, of June, and July-flowers.
> I sing of May-poles, Hock-carts, wassails, wakes,
> Of bride-grooms, brides and of their bridal-cakes.

The author of such well-known lines as 'Cherry ripe, ripe,
ripe I cry', Herrick was at his best describing the delights of
the countryside, but he also left a pleasing picture of his life
with his elderly housekeeper, Prudence Baldwin, with
whom he lived in his vicarage surrounded by pets of various
kinds:

> Here, here I live with what my Board,
> Can with the smallest cost afford.
> Though ne'er so mean the Viands be,
> They well content my Prew and me.
> Or Pea, or Bean, or Wort, or Beet,
> Whatever comes, content makes sweet:
> Here we rejoyce, because no Rent
> We pay for our poore Tenement:
> Wherein we rest, and never feare
> The Landlord, or the Usurer.
> The Quarter-day do ne'er affright
> Our Peacefull slumbers in the night.
> We eate our own and batten more,
> Because we feed on no man's score;
> But pitie those, whose flanks grow great,
> Swell'd with the Lard of others' meat.

In other verses he provided a charming picture of his
vicarage:

> Lord Thou hast given me a cell
> Wherein to dwell
> A little house whose humble roof

Is weather proof:
Under the spars of which I lie
Both soft and dry.
. . . .
Like as my parlour, so my Hall
And kitchen's small
A little buttery and therein
A little bin,
Which keeps my little loaf of bred
Unchipt, unflead:
Some brittle sticks of thorn or briar
Make me a fire,
Close by whose living coal I sit
And glow like it.

Heedless of the storm to come he glorified the old ways of country life detested by the Puritans:

For Sports, for Pagentrie and Playes,
Thou hast thy Eves and Holydayes . . .
Thy Wakes, thy Quintels, here thou hast,
Thy May-poles too with Garlands grac't:
Thy Morris-dance: thy Whitsun ale:
Thy Sheering-feast, which never faile.
Thy Harvest home; thy Wassaile bowle,
That's tost up after Fox i' th' Hole:
Thy Mummeries: thy Twelfe-tide Kings
And Queenes: thy Christmas revellings.

This same celibate cleric could also write of his real or imaginary loves in quite explicit terms, though sometimes less aptly than might be expected from experience of reality:

Fain would I kiss my Julia's dainty leg,
Which is as white and hairless as an egg.

During the time of the Commonwealth when he had been turned out of his living, not surprisingly, his verse turned to more sombre themes on occasions:

Men are suspicious; prone to discontent;
Subjects still loathe the present Government.

After preaching on Midsummer Day in 1647, Herrick was

abruptly supplanted by a Puritan weaver named John Syme. Happily, he returned again to his living at the Restoration in 1662 and lived on for a further twelve years, dying at the age of eighty-three in 1674. It is pleasant to know that he returned to his living and easy to imagine the general welcome he received from his old parishioners, although such was not always the case.

The period of the Civil Wars unfortunately brought out the extremists on both sides, as civil wars are wont to do. If it is accepted that they were as much religious as political in background, a backwash of the Reformation a hundred years previously, the unrest from which had been slowly growing, something of the bitterness of the time may be more easily understood. Moderate clerics of either Laudian or Puritan inclination must have been agreed that the Church required setting in order, that disorderly scenes at wakes, or church services, should not be permitted and that numerous churches required renovation. Broadly speaking the main differences were that the loyal clerics were in favour of conformity and stricter control of worship, while the Puritans were for greater freedom from control and plainer services, concentrating on the preaching of the sermon. The former favoured beautifying their churches with fine carvings, altar cloths and stained glass, while the latter were for barring vestments and whitewashing the church interiors.

The real clash, however, was not one of doctrine, or logic, but of temperament. There has always been a strain of puritanism in the British character and when carried to extremes it is not the most attractive of traits. The contrast between Philip Stubbs and Herrick epitomises the differing viewpoints. Stubbs inadvertently exposed the lewdness of his own mind in his ranting denunciation of the May Day revels, while Herrick's fresh verses depicted the village girls innocently dancing garlanded with flowers which were then hung in the church.

Extremists apart, there were of course men of genuine piety and reasonableness on either side unable by the exigencies of the times to remain neutral and forced to align themselves with one or other party. One of the more prominent Puritan nonconformist ministers was Richard Baxter, in reality a moderate in every sense. Although generally considered a Presbyterian he had no real objection to a mild form of Episcopalianism. Curate of Kidderminster in Worcestershire, a royalist stronghold, for some nineteen years he was subjected to continual persecution by supporters of the king. For a period he acted as chaplain to a regiment in the Parliamentary forces, yet he preached before Cromwell in favour of the monarchy and helped to bring about the Restoration.

Unable to accept either the offer of a bishopric or the Act of Uniformity in 1662, he was ejected from his living and subjected to further persecutions. At one point he was forced to appeal for protection from slanders to the Bishop of Worcester, John Earle. As rector of Bishopston in Wiltshire, Earle had himself been ejected by the Puritans and he responded generously to Baxter's plea, replying: 'I should be heartily sorry and ashamed to be guilty of anything like malignity and uncharitableness, especially to one of your condition, with whom, though I concur not perhaps in a point of judgement in some particulars, yet I cannot but esteem for your personal worth and abilities.'

Baxter was so moved by this that he wrote on the letter: 'O that they were all such!' Although he married Margaret Chalton in 1662 and drew great consolation from a wife eminently suited to his turn of mind, Baxter continued to be harassed and persecuted. After her death in 1681 he was accused of libelling the Church in his *Paraphrase of the New Testament*. In 1685 he appeared before the Chief Justice, the dreaded Sir George Jeffreys. In a travesty of justice, Judge Jeffreys commented: 'We have had to do with other sorts of persons, but we now have a saint to deal with; and I know how to deal with saints as well as sinners.'

It is said that Jeffreys proposed at first that Baxter, though now seventy and frail, should be whipped at a cart tail through the town, but in the event he was fined 500 marks and imprisoned for eighteen months until the fine was remitted. After the Act of Indulgence in 1687 he helped to bring about the downfall of James II and complied with the Act of Toleration under William and Mary. He died in 1691 at the age of seventy-six, by which time his worth had been recognised by all.

Baxter's career was one side of the picture. John Earle's was the other. There were numerous lesser clerics who suffered on either side, for with the civil wars and establishment of the Commonwealth and Protectorate several thousand loyalist incumbents were evicted from their livings, many to be imprisoned, or to die in poverty. With the Restoration and the Act of Uniformity in 1662 some two thousand clergymen who did not take the oath were evicted from their livings.

It was a period of really vicious disruption in the countryside and much of the deep-seated ill-feeling and bitterness engendered then persisted for many years, sometimes for generations. Inevitably the years of Puritan rule left their mark on the Church and on the country as a whole, both at local and national levels. Sunday in particular was no longer regarded as a day of freedom as it had been previously. The old wakes and festivals might be revived in places, but never again with quite the same carefree spirit of old. In some areas also the whole system of tithe-paying had become upset. There were, for example, instances when on the eviction of a loyalist incumbent the royalist parishioners refused to pay tithes to his supplanter, and even raided the tithe barns to provide for their ex-priest. Conversely nonconformists in after-years were often understandably reluctant to pay tithes to their Anglican incumbent. Laws might be passed to compel payments, but they were inevitably difficult and tiresome to enforce, causing even greater ill-feeling in the process. Individuals throughout the country, whether lay or clerical, always found ways to circumvent the law, or abide by the letter rather than the intent.

# 1

## The Rev. Ralph Josselin

### Puritan Farmer and Businessman: Essex

*I reckon that day a good day to me*

Despite the cataclysmic nature of the struggle which convulsed the nation, there were some clergymen who retained their livings throughout the period of the Civil War and the Restoration without the inconstancy attributed in song to the vicar of Bray. One such was the Rev. Ralph Josselin, who lived from 1616 to 1683. For the greater part of these years he kept a diary entitled: *A Thankfull Observacon of Divine Providence & Goodness towards Mee & a Summary View of My Life by Me Ralph Josselin.* This largely unselfconscious record casts many revealing sidelights on this troubled period.

The only son of a wealthy miller who lost much of his money farming, Josselin was educated at Bishops Stortford and Jesus College, Cambridge. Left in comparative poverty while still at Cambridge on his father's unexpected death, he spent two years as a schoolmaster in Bedfordshire before moving to Olney in Buckinghamshire where he was ordained and acted as curate. Here he married in 1640. Then, in March 1641, at the instigation of the Harlakenden family, who were related to Oliver Cromwell, he first visited Earls Colne in Essex, where he was to spend the rest of his life. He recorded:

*The road to Colchester framing the church tower at Earls Colne in Essex, much changed since the Rev. Ralph Josselin held the living in the seventeenth century.*

'I came over . . . to Mr. Rich. Harlakendens at the priory:
I was affected with that family exceedingly & the situation of
the Towne . . . I preach . . . they desired mee I would come
& live with them as their Minister: I . . . answered them, if
they would make the meanes & competency such as I could
live on, which I conceived was £80 per annum, I would
embrace; they gladly entertained it & valewed it thus to
mee:

| | | |
|---|---:|---:|
| Tithes they would make good at | £40 | 0s |
| Mr. R. Harlakenden: wood & money | 20 | 0 |
| His tenants in contribucon | 2 | 0 |
| Mr. Tho. Harlakenden | 3 | 0 |
| And towne contribucon | 15 | 0 |

The House, close, churchyard and the dues that
accrewed to the Minister, they conceived to bee worth £10
per annum, thus . . . I accepted . . .'

After they had 'passed all with the Bishop' Ralph Josselin
settled down happily in his ministry, although he very
quickly found that the townspeople of Earls Colne were
extremely backward in playing their part in the bargain. By
October he and his wife were established in a house in the
high street of the town and she soon afterwards gave birth to
a daughter, Mary. He also recorded:

'This Michaelmas, upon an Order of the House of
Commons to that purpose wee tooke downe all images &
pictures and such like glasses; thus the winter passed away a
time of hopes & yet sometimes feares . . .'

Already the tensions were beginning to build up throughout the country and with the outbreak of the Civil War in
1642 he noted:

'. . . about Midsummer wee began to raise private armes;
I found a musquett for my part . . . our poor people in
tumults arose & plundered divers houses, papists & others
. . . which I endeavored to suppresse . . .'

Surprisingly the years 1643 and 1644 seem to have been comparatively peaceful in that Puritan stronghold. In January 1644 he recorded:

'10th. The Arch Bishop, that grand enemy of the pouer of godlynes, that great stickler for all outward pompe in the service of God, left his head at Touer Hill London, by ordinance of parliament.'

To anyone of Puritan inclinations the death of Laud, their great oppressor, must have been a moment of great triumph and Josselin's comment was comparatively restrained.

In 1645 came the entry:

'June 10, 11, 12. I was out with our regiment: was marched to Walden, musterd. I sung Psalmes, prayd & spoke to our souldiers on ye Common at Waldon & also at Halsted . . . our souldiers resolute, some somewhat dissolute: the Collonel was pleased to honor mee to bee his Comrade [Colonel Harlakenden].'

Despite various alarms it comes as something of an anti-climax to read:

'Sept. 4. Returned home safe with our troops; no damage to any man, one horse shott in ye legge through a mistake; my horses eye hurt.'

In 1645 he bought a small farm and with this and other small speculations his affairs were beginning to prosper slowly. In 1646 he lost £16 he had invested in the cargo of a ship which was wrecked on the coast, but it is indicative of his careful judgement that this was the first loss he had made since his days at Cambridge. He recorded that although he owed £100 he was receiving about £20 a year rent for land. When offered the living of Thaxted he decided that he preferred to stay in Earls Colne.

In December 1646 he wrote:

'Troopes among us, very erroneous fellowes, but otherwise indifferent civill.'

With apparent satisfaction he noted:

'Dec. 25. People hanker after the sports and pastimes that

they were wonted to enjoy, but they are in many families weaned from them.'

The advent of the second Civil War between Parliament and the Army in 1648 brought renewed upsets. In June the Parliamentary forces marched on Colchester and he recorded:

'June 12. On Monday morning the enemy came to Colne, were resisted by our towne men. No part of Essex gave them so much opposition as wee did; they plundered us, and mee in particular, of all that was portable, except brass, pewter and bedding; I made away to Coggeshall and avoyded their scouts through providence . . . it is not much to part with any thing as wee suppose, God can give us a contented heart in any condicion . . .'

Early in 1649 he mirrored the feelings of many of every persuasion when he noted:

'Feb. 4. I was much troubled with the blacke providence of putting the King to death; my teares were not restrained at the passages about his death . . .'

Later in the month he was no doubt again voicing popular opinion:

'Feb. 18. Great dearth and want of all things. I gave 4d per pound for porke.' A few months later he noted also: 'May 20: great scarcity of all things, rye at 6s 8d bushel, butter at 7d a pound, cheese 6d, beefe 5d, lamb 7d.'

He was asked to subscribe against the present proceedings and dissent from the execution of the king, but with characteristic caution refused to commit himself. On the other hand he found time to subscribe to the Engagement, which read:

'I do declare and promise that I will be true and faithful to the Commonwealth of England as the same is now established, without a King, or House of Lords.'

He recorded this and gave his reasons for signing:

'Dec. 18. This day I rid to Waltham and 19 to Chelmsford where I subscribed the Engagement, the first in ye County of

Ministers and ye 13th man of ye County . . . as I considered
it stood with ye Covenent, while ye government actually
stood established and my faithfulness is not to create any
trouble, but seek ye good of ye Commonwealth.'

Ralph Josselin simply did not want any more trouble and
there must have been many throughout the country with a
similar philosophy. By this time he was in his mid-thirties
and was becoming increasingly shrewd in his dealings with
others as his diary demonstrates. On April 20th 1650 he
wrote:

'Bee cautious of speaking to Mr. Harlakenden in the point
of his royalties [grants of office, in this case from the
Commonwealth] for being intent on the proffits of them, he
takes it ill, as I found this day, which I hope shall learne mee
some prudence in the world. I would willingly bee a gainer
by other mens tempers.'

Some indication of his commercial ability may be had
from the entries in the same year:

'June 24. This morning I bought Smith's cow: her price
was £6.10s.0d. I also bought of him the pasture of Dagnall
till Michaelmas for £3.10s: he is to pay me the tithe which I
told him of, and to pay all towne taxes untill michaelmas. I
am to enter them on Wednesday. I borrowed the money of
Goodwife Math: 40s. I now paid him in hand: if I buy cowes
I am to putt them now on the ground: the Lord my God give
a blessing unto mee herein.

'June 27. This day I fetcht a cow from Westney's of
Halstead, it cost £6.5s: I had great trouble in ye cowes
unquietnes: God enters mee into many of my affayres with
trouble . . .

'Sept. 6. This day my cowes were driven away from
Smiths from off his ground with his, for rent by his landlady.
I apprehended it might have beene some trouble to mee; I
followed after them, overtooke them, and had my cowes
delivered quietly to mee . . .'

He also obtained the post of deputy schoolmaster for the

absentee holder of that office, Dr Wright, and this was worth £70 per annum to him so that, scarcely surprisingly, his affairs prospered. In 1652 at the age of thirty-seven, for the first time he recorded himself as being in credit to the sum of £114.5s. His diary mirrored his life with occasional mention of outside events. Thus in 1654 he noted:

'March 6. Wett day: rid to Colchester. I find some earnestly oppose Protector; others close with him on grounds that carry a faire face: the Lord keep my heart closely & wisely to retain the doves innocency.'

In January 1657 it appeared that Dr Wright, through whom he had obtained the post of schoolmaster, was seriously ill. He therefore noted with evident relief:

'Jan. 31. Heard certainly of Dr. Wright's hopeful recovery.

'Feb. 1. God good to mee this weeke in taking care of my livelyhood, in Dr. Wrights life, by whose death ye schoole had gone from mee, worth neare £70 yearly to mee, and besides the comfort to teach my children, the feare also of a bad neighbour.'

Unfortunately for Ralph Josselin, Dr Wright died in October and in November came the unwelcome news that the Earl of Oxford's chaplain, Dr Pullein, was interested in the appointment, although only if he failed to obtain a living which with Lord Oxford's backing he hoped to gain. Josselin duly recorded the sequence of events:

'Nov. 27. Dr. Pullein was with mee, shewed mee his grant from my Lord; he lost the living, for which I am sorry, and I the schoole; Gods will be done; I doe not find any trouble on my spirit in it; he desired mee to teach the schoole till spring for halfe the proffits; I consented; lord I blesse thee for that kindness and mercy.'

On December 3rd another entry indicated that hope was not yet extinguished as there was still a chance that Dr Pullein might after all obtain his living, hence Josselin the school. Although he expressed his Christian resignation, the psychological pressures must have been great as his next entry showed:

'Dec. 5. Riding over to the Earl of Oxfords to Bently hall, and speaking with Dr. Pullein, a full issue was put to that treaty about the schoole; I not having it, in which disposall of God I desire to bee satisfied, and sitt down contentedly, knowing that he will order and direct everything for good to mee; I was very sicke at night and vomited, which I judged a mercy to mee.'

In 1658 he wrote:

'Feb. 22. . . . this day Dr. Pullein here: he hired the Justices house and intends to come over very speedily; though the schoole bee a great losse unto mee, yet God will provide for mee . . .

'July 9. This day Dr. Pullein came to Towne: he is our schoolMr.

'July 12. Dismist my schollers to Dr. Pullein.'

As if of little importance, there followed shortly:

'Sept. 3. Cromwell died, people not much minding it.'

In 1659 his eldest son Thomas was sent to London to be apprenticed and in 1660 came a notable series of entries:

'June 3. Ye King returned in safety and with hopes of being a blessing to the nacon.

'June 6. Rid to lay claime to the Kings pardon before ye Maior of Colchester.

'June 10. A great calme in ye contry. The Kings proclamacon agst debaucht courses a cutt to the gentry of England; oh Lord make him a nursing ffather to thy people.

'July 22. Ministers pitifully put out of their livings while others advanced. Our schoolemaster Dr. Pullein said to bee made a Bishop of Londonderry . . . heard of threatenings against mee, but ye Lord is a sheild to mee who never sought the wrong of others.

'July 29. Our Dr. Pullein said to bee Arch Bp of Tuam . . . in Connaught.

'Aug. 12. The Arch Bp of Tuam with us: people wonderfully neglect the sabbath and yett God holds his hand.

'Aug. 26. Dr. Pullein now an Arch Bp being to remove from us, occasioned great feastings, which are vain tainting things to our minds. God in some measure abased my heart.'

Some idea of the tension at the time may be gleaned from the next entry:

'Aug. 29. Preacht at Colchester for Mr. Stockdale . . . signed the act of indemnity past. Talke as if the honest partie were in hazard of a massacre; I feare some jealous heartes are foolishly at worke; I cannot thinke such a wickednes. This day the King passed the act of pardon; I was glad I was so well employed on a day when so memorable an act was past.'

By the following year he was beginning to regain confidence and also finding certain aspects of the Restoration hard to tolerate:

'March 10, 1661. This day I heard and then saw the youth openly playing at catt on the green: I went up, rowted them; yr fathers sleeping in the chimmney corner: Lord heale through grace these disorders.

'March 17. Children very profane: their parents sitt at home and they play in the streets openly at catt and other sports.

'June 23. Said Bishops and their courts are coming in again. Lorde helps us to walke humbly & wisely.'

Although it was fairly obvious from his comments in his diary that he did not much like Dr Pullein, by this time translated to the archbishopric of Tuam, it could well be that his close acquaintance with him stood Josselin in good stead. In May 1662 the Act of Uniformity was passed and he recorded the events which followed thus:

'June 1. I had the Act of Uniformity sent mee.

'July 13. Reports as if the King would respitt the penalties on the Act of Uniformity as to himselfe for a time.

'Aug. 17. The last Sabbath of our liberty by the Act.

'Aug. 24. Some hopes given as if there would bee indulgence given to ministers for the present until the return of parliament.

'Aug. 31. All hopes of the suspension of the Act of Uniformity taken away. God good to mee in my freedome to preach, three ministers and multitudes of our christian neighbors hearing.

'Sept. 7. A quiet Sabbath, great droves of people flocke to heare.

'Nov. 9. New Ministers this day at Colne Engain, Mr. Symonds & at Cogshall Mr. Jessop: both of good report. and now I am left alone of the nonconformists, what God will doe with mee I know not.

'Nov. 12. A snowy bitter rainy windy morning in which I went to the Court [the Episcopal Court at Colchester] cited for procuracons [sums of money paid annually to the bishop or archdeacon by the parish priest]. Mine are as large as livings of £120 per yeare. I paid & returned well, blessed bee God: none of the nonconformists being cited appeared but onely my selfe: I reckon that day a good day to mee.'

The inconsistency of acknowledging the Bishop's Court, while claiming nonconformity, does not seem to have occurred to him. From this point onwards, however, Josselin gradually notes changes in his services amongst other diary entries. Thus in 1663, he recorded:

'May 30. This day our churchwardens brought in ye booke of common prayer which I used.'

In 1665 he wrote:

'26 March. Easter Day. 12 of us received ye sacrament of ye Lords supper publiquly for which I blesse God: I believe its 22 or 23 yeares since received on yt day and occasion.

'May 7. I began to expound things out of the church catechism for the information of youth.'

The great plague of 1665 and 1666 which affected London and many parts of the country so badly, passed Earls Colne safely. From this time onwards, however,

Josselin's family posed increasing problems. His sons were a sad disappointment to him. The eldest died comparatively young and unmarried. The younger, John, developed into a chronic alcoholic and was finally disowned. A further source of worry was finding proper suitors for his daughters and providing them with dowries. Outwardly, however, Josselin's life continued much in the pattern already clearly set. Two successive entries in 1669 showed where his main interests lay:

'July 9. Rid to Court [the Episcopal Court] whither summoned for not wearing the surplice; dismissed without fee.

'July 10. Made an end of haying for this year and my hay very good. God be praised for this mercy; it cost mee the least of any years mowing & making & inning not above 40s besides my own helpe.'

In 1670 his daughter Jane was married to a local tanner, worth 'about £500'. Josselin noted proudly:

'Aug. 30. My daughter Jane married to Jonathan Wood-thorp, our first marriage; the Lord bless them with his grace and favor, for porcon I am to give her £200; the clothes and wedding cost mee £10; she hath a prettie thing in joynture; blessed be God who hath thus provided for mee and mine; her plate & worke is worth £40 and shee hath in money £20.'

In 1672 he suffered his first attack of what he termed 'sciatica', probably phlebitis, which was to grow progressively worse over the years despite such attempts at curing it as taking the waters at Tonbridge Wells. With his various family worries, especially the behaviour of his drunken younger son John, his health deteriorated and on 25th January 1675 he recorded:

'Sensible this entred my 60 yeare: I grow an old man; my leg swels hard on ye calfe and so continueth in mornings.'

On September 19th of the same year he noted:

'This day wee had a parochial visitacion; some things

complained of, as the want of a surplice, in other things it was well.'

Regarding his son John he wrote:

'Oct. 15. My son the seat of drunknes. . . . I am resolved to leave him to thee oh God, only I will pray for him.'

For the next few years his thoughts revolved around marrying his daughters suitably and in particular his eldest daughter Mary. In 1679 in rather surprising conjunction he noted:

'May 16. An offer for Mary: God direct: I wore ye surplice.

'May 17. Rid to court, I avoided receiving article, through God's goodnes. I cast my care on him, he cared; the matter is the surplice, which I see no sin to use, & shall endeavor to live as quietly as may bee to the end of my race . . .'

There was also one final entry regarding the black sheep:

'Oct. 16. John married unknown to mee: God pardon his errors.'

In 1680 and 1681 Josselin's wife was ill, but in 1682 he entered:

'May 7. Wett: flouds this weeke: I could not stirre a plow: much soft corn spoild: I had a bad markett for corn: my family troubles continue, esp. a froward wife.'

There was however a cheerful note about the final entry in December that year:

'On the 25 at one of the clocke my friends came from London; the greatest chrismas I kept; yr being 2 young men, Mr. Day & Mr. Spicer, welwillers to my virgin daughters: wee had good society; 3 of them went away, the 29th, well satisfied.'

On 10th April 1683 his third daughter, Mary, 'being somewhat above 25 years old', was married 'to Mr. Edward Day . . . a tallow chandler of St. Martins. He is his father's only child, a man of good estate & godly conversacon. I gave her for porcon my house I dwell in & land belonging yr to worth £400 and an £100.'

On May 6th he recorded another satisfactory marriage:

'Mr. Spicer married my youngest daughter Mrs. Rebekah: I rid down in her coach & performed it for them . . . I was joyd God had so well provided for her. I gave her £500 down & with my blessing sent her away.'

By this time he must have been failing fast and wrote in July:

'July 7. My wife returned safe from London, my six sons & daughters came to the coach with her in health.'

With all his daughters by this time married and living in London, even if 'in health', he no doubt felt he had successfully completed his life's work. Even so his final entry on July 29th was typical:

'Wee begun harvest July 27 reaping and mowing. God send us . . .'

There, save for a broken sentence or two the diary ends. It was coupling God and his harvest which suited Ralph Josselin in life and therefore seems most suitable as the last entry in his diary.

His merits as a priest may not have been obviously outstanding, but his survival alone was note-worthy. As a farmer he was undoubtedly successful.

# 2

## The Rev. George Turnbull

### Early Presbyterian Minister: East Lothian

*This night my gowt . . . seized me again*

Another reverend diarist, whose life overlapped with that of Ralph Josselin, was George Turnbull, minister of Alloa in Clackmannan from 1688 to 1699 and of Tyninghame in East Lothian from 1699 to 1731. Born in 1657 he died at the advanced age of eighty-seven in 1744, having been a Presbyterian minister for fifty-six years throughout a momentous period in Scots history and in the history of the Presbyterian Church. Although the Restoration of Charles II in 1662 was as warmly welcomed in Scotland as in England, the events which followed were by no means so peaceful.

After appointing a Privy Council, under the direction of the Duke of Lauderdale as Secretary, normally resident in London, the king paid little or no attention to further events in Scotland. Episcopalianism and the rule of the bishops, anathema to Presbyterians, was re-established and the appointment of ministers by patronage was reintroduced, although numerous Presbyterian ministers refused to conform. Persecution of the covenanting cause of the non-conformist Presbyterians grew steadily more intense throughout Charles II's reign. The rising of Rullion Green in 1666 and the battle of Bothwell Bridge in 1679, when the Covenanters on each occasion were soundly defeated,

*A view of the Bass Rock and the East Lothian coastline from Tyninghame today which the Rev. George Turnbull would have recognised as virtually unchanged since the eighteenth century.*

merely gave rise to further oppression and with the advent of James VII and II to the throne in 1685 came the period grimly known as 'the killing time'. The Declaration of Indulgence in 1687 allowed freedom of worship, but it was not until after the coronation of William III and Mary in 1689 that the official Church of Scotland was recognised as Presbyterian in 1690.

George Turnbull's diary is refreshingly devoid of the intense soul-searching of so many similar records, but unfortunately it does not cover the period beyond 1704. The next twenty-seven years of his ministry at Tyninghame and the thirteen years after his retirement on resigning his charge in 1731 at the age of seventy-four are left a blank. Enough of his way of life is recorded before 1704, however, to form a clear picture of the man.

Although he came from a covenanting background and one of his sons was later Moderator, he was the first of his family to become a minister. His grandfather, after whom he was named, was a baker of some substance in Edinburgh in the first half of the seventeenth century. During the years of persecution from 1679 to 1687 the entire family suffered to a greater or lesser degree. In 1679 the grandfather was heavily fined for allowing conventicles to be held on his property and his sons, George Turnbull's father and uncle, were forced to flee for refuge to Holland. Four years later George himself followed them to study divinity at Utrecht University.

With this background the somewhat condensed early diary entries are more readily understood. Bought in London on 10th August 1687 on his return to Britain and priced at one shilling the diary is entitled: *A Diary or Day Booke, containing such remarkable providences and passages of my life as for spirituall and civil reasons I thought fitt to observe, and sett doune there date. — Pas 90th, 12th.*

The beginning is straightforward enough:

'I was born at Edenr. Decr. 7th 1657 and was baptised

there by Mr. John Sterline; was educatt att the latine school under Mr. Da. Skuigh[1] and att the colledge of Edenr. under Mr. William Paterson and received my degree Aug. 18 1675.'

After his father's flight to Holland in 1679 he took over the management of the small rented farm on which the family lived. When they were finally evicted from this for nonconformity he saw the family settled in the village of Blackness and noted laconically:

'I went for Holland and arrived att Rotterdam July 2 1683, having been five days at sea betwixt it and Boro-stounness.[2] July 19, Ditto I went up to the university of Utrecht and there I studied divinity.'

By this time in his twenty-fourth year, George Turnbull was now decided on his life's work and for the next four years he appears to have remained in Holland contentedly enough, until news of the Declaration of Indulgence arrived. In December 1687 he noted preaching in Delft, then he wrote in the diary which he had obtained earlier that year:

'Fryday, Decr. 30th. I shipped aboard a ship, John Andreson, Master, for London, where next Thursday, Janry. 5th I arrived safe.'

He was not long in getting himself ordained. He recorded:

'Moonday, Janry. 23. Preached for tryall in order to ordination on that Scripture, act 10, 34.

'Febry. 9. I was ordained a minister of ye gospell by imposition of hands. ministers concerned. Mr. Geo Hamilton, abram Hume, Nicol Blaky Rott. Traill, James Fraser, James Broun, David Blair, Thomas Douglass, John Herbert. witnesses Lord Kerdross, Coltness, Moriston, Mr. Stevinson and others.'

Finally came the no doubt welcome entry:

'Saturday 26th. I came to Scotland and stayed at Blackburne in the merce[3] till moonday.

'Sunday 27. I lectured on pas. 19: thence I came to ye queensferry moondays night, thus god again restored me to my freinds and native countrey.'

Throughout the rest of 1688 he was extremely busy, although without a parish, remaining an unattached minister, performing a great many baptisms and marriages. It is clear that at this period the few Presbyterian ministers were in great demand and the assumption must be that the Episcopalian ministers, by comparison, were finding very little to do. For the next two years, until September 1690, the same pattern of events continued. Then he was called to Alloa and 'accepted of it'. Finally he recorded:

'Fryday 26th. Mr. Alexr. Douglass, minister of Logie, preaching and all the presbitry of Sterlin with some assistants concurring, I was admitted minister of Alloway.'

For the next eleven years as minister of Alloa, George Turnbull was immensely busy as a single week's extract from his diary will demonstrate:

'Apr. 12 1691. Lectured and preached at ditto [Alloa].

'13th — I marryed a couple from dumblan.[4]

'14th — Another couple from Tillicutry.

'15th — Baptised a child at airth.

'16th — Baptised 3 children and marryed two couple at Logie.'

As the numbers desiring to be married and baptised eased somewhat he was quite as busy preaching and lecturing and attending to the needs of his parish, occasionally attending meetings of his Presbytery or the General Assembly, or preaching in the Tron Kirk in Edinburgh. The steady increase in the numbers of Presbyterian ministers undoubtedly eased the pressure on those already ordained, but even so it is clear that throughout his ministry in Alloa, Turnbull was working under considerable pressure with little in the way of relief.

While away on Presbytery business in January 1695 he recorded:

'on Thursday (10th) I was all night att Sauchy Glass.'[5]

In February he recorded equally unrevealingly:

'Thursday 28. — I came from Edenr., and was att Sauchy, thence next day home.'

In April there was the bald entry:

'12th — Being Fryday, Mr. Rott Rule, minister att Sterlin marryed me and Elizabeth Glass[6] my wife togither in the house of Sauchy.'

He made no mention of the fact that at the same time his wife's sister Grissel was married to Mr Thomas Buchanan, minister of Tulliallan. Presumably after the double ceremony there were fairly lengthy celebrations, but no mention is made beyond the entry:

'19th — I brought my wife home.'

Although Turnbull had reached the mature age of thirty-eight before their marriage, it seems to have been extremely successful. His first son, William, was born in April of the following year, 1696, and six more sons and two daughters followed at intervals up to 1714. Occasional visits thereafter were noted to his sister-in-law at Tulliallan and in 1697 his brother-in-law, Adam Glass, was ordained minister of Aberlady in East Lothian. Through his marriage he gained not only a happy family background but also some influential connections amongst his wife's relations.

In April 1688 Turnbull fell ill and remained unwell for the rest of the year, appearing close to death in January 1689 and still unable to preach in April, when he recorded a change of doctor and noted rather hopelessly:

'Aprile 2d. Mr. Robin preacht for me.'

Then came an obviously unexpected entry.

'Apr. 15th. Mr. Forrest's[7] letter came to my hand, bearing a call the parock of Tuningham was preparing for me. I did and doe still lay that affair entirely befor the Lord.'[8]

In May he noted:

'Wedensday, May 3. — I supplicatt the pbitry for a trans-portability in regard my health could not bear up under the weight of my psent charge. out of pity and compassion to me they granted it upon the matter . . .

'13th May. I heard my call to Tuningham was duly and harmoniously perfected.'

He was then placed on a goat's milk diet, from which it may be inferred that he was suffering from stomach ulcers, probably caused by overwork and strain. He recorded somewhat gloomily, with a Lowland bias:

'Moonday May 15th. I tooke journey in order to get my goat milke dyett; lodged that night at Coldoch; next day I came to my quarters which was in John Grahams house att the bridge-end aberfoyl; the place is pretty pleasant, close by the Forth waterside, att the foot of Craigmor, betwixt which and the water there is a strath very proper for walking; the people rude and ignorant, but not unkind after the highland way. pvidence having in ane unexpected manner set me up hither for my milke in the midst of my barbarous and disaffected neighbours I looked to god, waitted and doe waitt for his protection and blessing to the means.'

On June 4th he recorded more happily:

'I bless the lord my milke still aggried with me, my neighbours still kind and my family well att home . . .'

On the 11th of June he recorded his opinion:

'This people of aberfoyll no untractable people, there psent minr. silly.'[9]

On the 19th of June after a month of goat's milk he returned home sufficiently recovered to start preaching again. On the 30th he noted:

'Mr. Logan of St. Ninians by commission from the pbtry intimatt to the heritors and elders that I was desiring a transportability on account of my health; they all professed great unwillingness to part with me.'

From then onwards everything went smoothly. On July 30th the Presbytery met and it was agreed that he should be allowed to accept the first call. Thus it can have come as little suprise when he recorded:

'Wedensday 16th August. Did Mr. Brown, minister of Spot, in the pbitry of dumbar, with two elders from

Tuningham, produce before the pbitry of sterlin a call to me from Tuningham, wch I received and tooke to consideration.'

On September 10th he noted:

'I preacht in Tinningham church for the first time . . .'

On the 13th of September he added:

'. . . I accepted of Tinningham call . . .'

The day of his admission was decided on as the 26th of September and he described this important event in his life very fully:

'Tuesday 26th. Mr. John Forrest preacht on coll 4.17 and the wholle presbitry of dumbarr being psent, except Mr. da. Clunny, minr att Cockburnspath, I was admitted minr at Tinningham, Sir Robert Sinclair of stevenson and John sheriff chamberlan receiving me in the Earle of Haddingtons name, Mr. Matthew red[10] minr att north Berwicke, in name of Sir George Sowty of Begonn[11], Rott jackson of Lochhouses for himself, which are all the heritors of that paroch; and all the Elders. severall minrs, and gentlemen strangers present. all this time my mind was in great perplexity, my spirit in bonds, rackt to know what was sin or diuty; the desolation of poor alloway paroch was grivous to me. O that god may provide well speedily for them.

'The same day of my admission the pbitry also visited the manse; we all dined in the Earle of Haddingtons house.'

On the 15th of October he preached his farewell sermon at Alloa and recorded the hope that 'the lord provide speedily and well for them', although it was not in fact to be fulfilled for a further five years. His furniture and belongings were then transported by boat to North Berwick and thence to Tyninghame. For the next thirty-one years his life was to lie in the comfortable lush lands of East Lothian, rather than the starker area around Alloa.

A more domestic note followed early in February:

'twesday 13th. About two in ye morning . . . was my wife brought to bed of a daughter, who, on Friday 16th, was baptised in the name of Marion by Mr. John Forrest, minr att preston-kirke. . ., My wife recovered pretty well, only her breasts very sore . . .

'25 . . . This weeke was sone George very sick of a feavar, as also my wife of very sore breasts. it pleased god mercifully to recover both.'

In between numerous notes of his ministerial duties and minor domestic matters there was a significant comment on the effects of the Darien disaster on the Scots' nation:

'Thursday 28th March. Being a nationall fast day for our psent sins and calamitys. pticularly our loss att Darien . . .'[12]

In July he recorded:

'This moneth was very windy and dry weather . . . owr heats and animositys continue; many enter into a resolve agst all forreign cloth and all french wines; this displeases the govtt. about this time captn campbell . . . comes to Edenr. from darien and affirms the surrender of it by treaty to ye spaniards.'

Although busy about his parochial duties it is noticeable that he was also more socially engaged than in Alloa. The entertainment offered in East Lothian amongst his aristocratic neighbours was undoubtedly of a much higher standard than he had been accustomed to in Clackmannan. This was not always to the good. In July 1700 he recorded:

'On the wedensday 24 I tooke a very severe colicke for wch I blamed a solyn goose,[13] a part whereof I had eat at the my lord Bellhavens house[14] the day before.'

The transition to the flesh-pots of East Lothian must have caused considerable prickings of conscience for in mid-August he noted:

'About this time I had many fears and doubts lesst I had erred and sinned in leaving the paroch of Alloway; lord clear them and provide mercifully for that people.'

Nevertheless the social round continued and took its toll. In October of the same year he wrote:

'Moonday 14th. My brother in law mr adam Glass and his

wife came here and stayed till Wedensday. that day we
dined at Smeiton, and went at night to Stevenson, next day
to Ormiston to visit my old Lady Haddington, where my
wife felt unwell and I believe miscarryed, she not knowing
she was with child; Friday we returned safe home blessed be
god.'

It is not perhaps surprising after the social round he was
enjoying and the amount of work in which he was engaged
that he found an old ailment recurring. On the 18th of
September 1701 he noted:

'This night my gowt, after two full years intermission,
seized me again, my pain was violent till the sabbath
morning.'

This was, however, followed shortly by better news:

'Saturday Septr. 27th. About six in the morning was my
wife brought to bed of a fourth son; he was baptised next
day being the lords day in the afternoon in the church by the
name of Thomas by mr Will Hamilton, minr at Whytekirke
. . . my gowt still continued.'

In March of 1702 he recorded the death of William III and
the accession of Queen Anne, noting with foreboding: 'what
god may bring out of this great change time must resolve;
but sad things seem to be threatned. . . . This weeke I tooke
the gowte in my right foot, where I never had it before, and
it qtinued with me some time, disabling me from preaching
two sabbaths.'

After noting the events in Parliament, when the Duke of
Hamilton, leader of the Jacobite party, led a walk-out of
some eighty members, whereupon the remainder continued
with their business, Turnbull, like many others, was plainly
somewhat perturbed by events. He wrote:

'Fryday July 3. Meditating on publike affairs I thought I
saw plainly a design laid to bring in the prince of wales and
yt severall in both partys acted in concert for that end, while
honeste men on both sides knew nor suspected nothing of
it; how far the court is qcerned time will discover; but our

talk of grievances under the late kings reign, our shyness to establish the succession, and complaints of pjudice done us by the English, and wishing to be disjoined even when ane union is treated of, are all preludes of the scene.'

In November he recorded:

'. . . the commissioners nominatt for ane union betwixt the two nations meet Tuesday novr 10 att London . . . but parted without concluding any thing, neither side being serious in the matter.'

He was not afraid to make his own views plain, however, when the opportunity came his way to do so publicly, as is shown in his entry:

'Wedensday 18th Nov. Att dunbar, being a pbitry day, I was chosen modr. that day we all tooke the oaths to Queen ann before the magistrats of dunbar. I as modr. first praying and then bespeaking the magistrats thus: — Gentlemen, magistrats of this city. We own Queen ann as our lawfull soveraign and sieing we have ptection under her govtt we reckon itt our diuty to swear alleadgance to her maj., being required so to do by lawfull authority. and we are also encouraged to this because her maj. has taken the coronation oath, and entered upon the govtt according to the claim of right and upon these terms we swear and subscribe.'

Early in 1703 tragedy struck the Turnbull household. He noted:

'On Thursday (Febry.) 11th in the evening Lord Binny[15] grew ill of a scarlet feavar, but soon recovered.

'Next fryday 19th my son William, and on the saturnday my daughter marion were both seized with a feavar; marions proved to be a scarlett feavar and she recovered soon; but william sickned more and more.

'Moonday. My son williams feavar encreased . . . and that night grew worse. on Twesday morning very early I sent for provost Edgar apothecary in Hadington, and Mr. Brown minr. of spot, both persons of known skill. about ten of the cloake they came. after they had seen the child and qsidered his case dovs[16] were applyed to his soles, and a blistering plaister to his neck, and a cordial julep given him now and then . . .'

Perhaps not surprisingly the six-year-old child grew worse in the night and died the following day. Both Turnbull and his wife were greatly affected and he recorded one of the few introspective entries in his diary on the subject, blaming his security over the past few years. He wrote:

'the child being much, alace I fear too much beloved by me, his death did sorly afflict me and the poor loving mother no less.'

When his daughter had a relapse, however, it was notable that he sent for another doctor, recording in early March:

'This weeke my daughter marion relapsed into a feavar. I sent for doctor Sinclar. the lord blessed the means, and she recovered.'

He too recovered from this tragedy in his family life and was soon back in his parochial routine with even greater fervour then before. Presbytery meetings and parochial duties kept him busy but he noted political developments in May with some foreboding when it seemed to him that a meeting of the Scots' Parliament was crowded with peers who had not sat since the Revolution and now were intending to promote Episcopalianism once again. He attended a meeting of the Kirk Commission the following day, 7th May, aimed at countering this tendency.

In July he noted a recurrence of his gout for some weeks, but a happier event occurred in August and the entry for the 6th of August read:

'About twelve of the cloake in the day my wife was delivered of her fifth son, who next lords day 8th of Aug. was baptised in the church of Tyningham by the name of William by Mr. John Shaw minr. of Lesly who preacht for me yt day on song 5 last; I called this boy William also in testimony of the lords kindness, who having taken away a son gave me another for him.'

His parochial duties and attendance at the General Assembly occupied him fairly fully, interrupted by occasional attacks of gout although there was noticeably less in the way of social gatherings after his first son William's death. In May 1704, however, his family occupied his thoughts somewhat, for he noted:

'Wedensday May 31. I preacht at Spott in the afternoon on psa 51.17 being ye fast day befor the sacrament.

'This same day my son George fell into a well in the town, but was mercyfully pserved and gott owt again; a mercy not to be forgotten.

'This day also was my son Willy weaned.'

In August he returned to his old parish and noted with pleasure:

'2nd. Being wedensday I preacht att Tillyallan on luke 12.1. Thursday I went to alloway to visit my old flock now again happily planted with an other minister Mr. John Logan transported from Killmadock to them, where I mett with my people in much love, joy and sorrow at once . . .'

At least his conscience was clear at last and on the 15th of September he recorded with evident satisfaction and happiness:

'The sacrament day I preached in the forenoon on luke 3.4 there were seven full tables. Mr. starke minr. att stention preached in the afternoon within and Mr Hary shaw minr. att Cockburnspath without in the afternoon. . . . It was a sweet gospell day and most pleasant weather, god follow it with a rich and plentyfull blessing.'

The final entry in the diary is for December 1704 and reads:

'31. Fornoon, preached on psa 148.7 and in the afternoon on the sixth comand.

'The weeke befor my son Thomas tooke a slight feavar, but it pleased god it soon passed over.'

Thus, coupling together his parochial duties and his son's

fever with God's will, the diary ends. He was to continue as minister of Tyninghame for the next twenty-seven years,[17] only resigning in September 1731 with advancing years and infirmity. Conscientious and serious to the point of lacking humour, a martyr to occasional attacks of gout, possibly an occupational affliction in that hard-drinking age, a shrewd enough observer of the political scene, a fond parent and husband, with a good wife behind him, he stands out as a model Presbyterian minister of his time.

# NOTES

1  Probably an ejected Presbyterian minister acting as teacher as many did, although subject to a fine or imprisonment if caught.
2  Bo'ness.
3  About twenty miles from Berwick in the parish of Cockburnspath, the property of Robert Brown a staunch Covenanter.
4  Dunblane.
5  In the parish of St. Ninians in Stirlingshire.
6  Sister of the incumbent of St. Ninians.
7  Minister of Prestonkirk, East Lothian.
8  The fact that his brother-in-law, Adam Glass, minister of Aberlady, East Lothian had married Helen Hamilton, a relation of the Earl of Haddington, owner of Tyninghame and that his wife's mother was related to Sir John Sinclair of Stevenson, East Lothian, could have helped.
9  The minister, Mr William Fisher, had been appointed Episcopal minister in 1696 by the Marquis of Montrose and due to his influence remained there until his death in 1723, the last Episcopal minister to hold a charge in Scotland after the Revolution.
10  Reid.
11  Suttie of Balgone.
12  The Darien disaster. The scheme for the formation of a Scottish colony at Panama, brainchild of William Paterson founder of the Bank of England, backed by Scottish capital foundered because of the climate, Spanish opposition and lack of English support. Cause of much anti-English feeling.
13  Gannets, bred on nearby Bass Rock, and regarded as a delicacy.
14  Biel, near Tyninghame. Lord Belhaven was a strong opponent of the

Union and no doubt had some trenchant comments to make on Darien.

15  Lord Binning, then aged five, eldest son of the Earl of Haddington.

16  Dovs were probably a concoction of coltsfoot leaves. Medicine at this time still aimed at dealing with the humours of the body and applications of heat and cold at extremities of the body were still standard treatment to drive out the evil humours supposedly causing the fever.

17  He was to have a second daughter born in 1706 and two more sons, Andrew and Robert, born in 1711 and 1714 respectively. Of his nine children seven survived, two daughters and five sons. Apart from George, the eldest remaining son, who became Professor of Philosophy at Aberdeen University, all the other sons became ministers and Thomas, born in 1701 at Tyninghame became Moderator in 1758. There can be little doubt that George Turnbull played his part in the rebuilding of the Presbyterian Church after the Revolution in more ways than one.

# 3

## The Rev. James Clegg

### Peak District Minister and Physician: Derbyshire

*Lord humble mee, give mee zeal, blow the fire*

Another Presbyterian country divine and diarist overlapping with George Turnbull was the Rev. Dr James Clegg, who ministered to his flock and practised as a physician as well over a wide area around his parish of Chapel-en-le-Frith in the Peak District of Derbyshire from 1703 to 1755. Aged seventy-six at his death, he led a remarkably active life, travelling very considerable distances on horseback, often in appallingly bad conditions.

Born on the 20th of October 1679 in the village of Shawfield close to Rochdale in Lancashire, the son of a clothier of the same name, Clegg's mother was a 'zealous dissenter'. Educated locally at various schools, he ended his studies with a year at Manchester at the age of nineteen. The following year he started preaching without authority and continued until invited in 1703 to accept the position of minister at Chapel-en-le-Frith at the age of twenty-four. To start with he acted as tutor to the sons of a Mr Bagshaw at Ford Hall near Malcalf and he was later ordained by a laying on of hands of the neighbouring ministers. He married a Miss Anne Champion of Edale on a stipend of £20 a year, and was thus forced to take on a farm at Stodhart, near

*The Presbyterian church at Stodhart, near Chapel-en-le-Frith in the Peak District, little changed from the mid-eighteenth century when the Rev. Dr James Clegg preached there, although now close to a main road and railway.*

Chapel-en-le-Frith, remaining at Stodhart Hall for the rest of his life.

His diary begins on March 16th 1729, thus covering in detail only the last twenty-five years of his life; however, he fortunately took the trouble to fill in the background himself and explained his reasons:

'Being now through the mercy of God in the 50th year of my life and having passed through many changes, conversed with many persons, been concerned on many affairs, and had considerable experiences by which I either have or might have learned some wisdom, I have determined to leave behind me a short account of the most remarkable passages of my life, only for the private use of such of my children as may survive me, from which by ye Grace of God they may possibly learn to escape many of the errors I have committed . . .'

The folio book of two hundred and sixty-five pages which resulted from this intention was in fact a detailed diary of his life, dealing with his parish work, his visits to the sick, details of their symptoms, illnesses and cures, or deaths, his sermons, farm work, family incidents, the births, marriages and deaths of local importance and his personal life. Although he claimed to start his diary only when he was fifty, it is quite clear that he had previously been in the habit of jotting down notes of events for a number of years, since many of the early entries have all the earmarks of being written at the time noted. Thus in the entry for 'Decr. 21st 1708', then aged twenty-eight, he wrote:

'This day I preached a funerall sermon from Job 19.25 in which I fear I affected more elegance of speech than was suitable to ye capacities or wants of my hearers. My heart hath been harder and my performance more lifeless and cold than they were of late. Lord humble mee, give mee zeal, blow the fire!'

The entries in the early years are sparse. In September 1721 he recorded the effects of smallpox on the district. He noted the deaths of entire local families from what at that time was one of the worst scourges in Europe. At this time he was already acting as an unqualified physician and on occasions with considerable success. For instance he noted:

'Nov. 1722; Mr. Richardson, an Excise man nr. Buxton, a serious young man, was seized with ye small pox. When I came to him I prescribed a womit which succeeded well. Ye small pox appeared on ye 4th day of ye confluent kind and very malignant with many purple spots intermixed. On the 12th day ye 2nd feavar was very high and on ye following days he was delirious. I prescribed opiates and alexipharmicks and 2 episparick plaisters. Through Gods assistance he recovered.'

He was invited to preside as a physician as far afield as London by distracted relatives who had evidence of his ability to effect cures locally, but, as he was the first to admit, he was by no means always successful, although he seems to have had a high percentage of cures. Proof of his growing reputation, both as a preacher and as a physician, as well as his simple attitude to life and his utter faith in God are all found in an entry for 1728.

'June 3rd. That night I found a messenger from the Congregation in Newcastle in Staffordshire to invite me to remove thither by ye offer of about 60 pounds per annum. This is more by half yn I have here, but that is what I must not be governed by. Ye people here dont use me well, but I hope I am of some use, especially to ye rising generation; and God hath hitherto very comfortably provided for me. I have not the least reason to distrust him for ye future, and I am determined to spend ye remainder of my life where I think I can do him ye best service.'

From this stage onwards the entries proliferate and it is clear he started to keep his diary seriously. A series in August show that his life was not all work and give an indication of his social life:

'Aug. 23rd. At home till the evening, then good old Mr. Finch minister at Norwich, sent for me and I enjoyed a very pleasant and profitable converse with him till 9 at night . . .

'August 25th. Preached twice on Cal.6.9. Catechised twice. Had two gentlemen with me in the evening, one from London, the other from Rye in Sussex.

'August 28th. At home all day; had twenty reapers, the wind exceeding high occasions the loss of much corn.'

Because he was not professionally qualified it is clear that at times James Clegg felt irked at not being able to insist on a treatment that he felt sure could effect a cure. He had initially not applied for a medical degree because of the expense involved. When he was threatened with a prosecution by the Ecclesiastical authorities for practising without a licence, however, he finally decided to approach a Scots university where a degree could be obtained by producing testimonials from practising physicians and paying the necessary fees.

An initial application to Edinburgh University was unsuccessful, whereupon he applied to Aberdeen University. In October 1729 came the quietly triumphant entry:

'Being this month created Doctor of Physick by a Diploma Medicum from the University of Aberdeen in North Brittain upon the Testimonials and Recommendations of Dr. Nettleton of Halifax, Dr. Dixon of Bolton and Dr. Latham of Finderne I think it is now proper to keep a more exact account of my patients, their diseases, ye remedies prescribed and the event, depending above all things on the Divine blessing for success.'

The variety of his life as a doctor and farmer, as well as minister, are well illustrated in an entry for July 24th 1730:

'Visited several sick persons about me, and was very busy amongst my haymakers. We got a good deal into ye barn very good. At night I went to Chappel[1] to seek for mowers.'

Nor was he prepared to leave everything to God, when swift action on his part was called for; as for instance in the same year:

'Dec. 17th. Heard that an execution was served on George Thornhills goods, sent for a cow he had of mine in haste and got her. This wretched condition his unclean life and continued intemperance hath brought him and his numerous family into.'

Yet the following year he was perfectly capable of indicating his belief in the Almighty in quite trivial connections with no sense of incongruity and with absolute conviction:

'May 14th. Mr. White gave me two guineas for advice and attendance on his wife. Thus Providence sends us in supplies.'

The entries during September and October indicate the variety of his life at this time of year:

'Sept. 7th. At home most of the day, overseeing ye reaping and leading of my wheat.

'Sept. 14th. I was invited to Park Hall and dined there with the Vicar of Glossop and his wife. My wife was with me and we returned well pleased with our entertainment and cheerful company.

'Sept. 15th. I was up pretty early and went out to meet Mr. Bagshaw and other friends at Small Dale to course hares. Several gentlemen with us, and had what they called good diversion, but to me its far from being as diverting as formerly.

'Oct. 7th. I spent the forenoon with my brother in shooting.

'Oct. 9th. Sent my man to Manchester for 4 Scotch cows.'

It is a curious point that although Dr Clegg had four sons and three daughters there are not many entries concerning them. He was undoubtedly a good father and very concerned for their welfare, but his entries about them were sometimes strangely offhand, as for instance:

'Nov. 12th. At night my son James came to us; he had been pursuing a servant maid that overran him.[2] He found her at Hope and in his passion[3] treated her ill, for which he is likely to come into trouble and deserved it.'

Yet he was prepared to go to endless trouble, not only for his own family, but for the families of members of his flock, or of friends or patients. Less than ten days later came the entry:

'Nov 21th. I met an emissary of ye Church of Rome at Sheffield. Some of that persuasion had seduced the daughter of Luke ffurness to that persuasion, and at ye request of the father I promised to meet any of that party and debate ye matters in controversy before ye daughter and other witnesses. The debate lasted near five hours; about 20 were present. Most of the company were fully satisfied, but ye young woman seemed obstinate after all. I had many fears about this dispute, lest a good cause should suffer through bad management on my side, but God assisted me and I had reason to be thankful.'

In 1733, however, there were three examples of his concern for his own family, which speak for themselves:

'April 26th. This morning my dear daughter Ann was married to Samuel Waterhouse. May the blessing of God be on them and make them blessings to each other and to all that are about them.

'June 10th. I preached twice. Expounded in the morning and catechised twice as usual. Much spent, but far more afflicted at night when son James came from Manchester and brought with him my son Joseph whom his master has turned out on account of his intemperance and injustice to him. This filled our poor family with unspeakable grief. We have reason to look on it as ye greatest affliction that ever came upon us.

'Sept 5th. I sent for daughter Ann, but she was prevented by a misfortune; an horse she had borrowed was hurt. I went to Heafield to agree the matter; but it must be much to their loss. May God sanctifie it to them.'

The following year, 1734, three further entries show his

feelings for his daughter Ann:

'March 6th. I had 5 teams from Chinley side to plow for us and we had a very favourable day. I rid over to see Katherine Brocklehurst at Overton, who is ill of an ague. Called on Francis Thomason and returned at even and went to bed much fatigued, but about midnight was called up by a messenger to my daughter at Heafield who was not expected to continue til I could come to her, and I set out and found her weak indeed but some little recruited.

'March 8th I rid over to Heafield again on the same account and had some little hope that Ann might recover . . .

'Aug. 9th. I rid over to Heafield to see my daughter. I paid her husband 20 pounds, which with what they had before makes 50 pounds — the portion I promised her.'

He was not a man to put up with wrongdoing in any form and sternly rebuked any backsliders in his flock as the following indicates:

'Oct. 31st 1734. Peter Wood came up to consult me what to do about his wife. Divine Providence hath at last discovered that she has for some years lived in adultery with a wicked wretch called Will Fox who had before debauched Ellen Ward. This is likely to bring on us and the good ways of God very great reproach. She formerly behaved well, was catechised and admitted to the Lords' Supper, and I had good hopes of her, but I hear the love of strong liquors hath ruined her.

'Nov. 16th. Went to Peter Wood's and according to my ability reproved and admonished his wife laying open the heinousness of her crime. She expressed much sorrow and contrition. I sharply reproved the maid Priscilla for concealing the wickedness so long, then returned to my work and was obliged to sit up late.

'Nov. 17th. I preached both parts of ye day from 2 Thes 3.1 and at night publickly expressed our detestation of the wickedness committed by W. Fox and Alice Wood, warning ye congregation to avoid him, and declaring her suspended from the Lord's Table till we had grounds to hope that her repentance was sincere.'

Although by his own confession not always of even temper, he was, notwithstanding, frequently called in to settle disputes and act as peacemaker between his parishioners and others, as for instance in December 1739:

'Dec. 3rd. Set out for Castletone to put an end to ye controversy between Mrs Hall and Staveley and did finish it, blessed be God! but not without difficulty.'

An entry soon afterwards recorded good news of his son Joseph, who had earlier been discharged as an apprentice for drunkenness.

'Dec. 14th. At night my brother John Clegg called on us on his return from London and lodged with us . . . and brings us very comfortable tidings from my son Joseph, for which I desire to be truly thankful. I once was afraid of great griefs and trouble in that child, but am now encouraged to hope for matter of rejoycing.'

In view of the amount of infectious diseases with which he was in contact (e.g. '1737 Sept. 13th. Called to William Howard . . . dangerously ill of ye Cholera Morbus.'), and the total lack of hygiene of the times, it is remarkable how healthy Dr Clegg and his family seem to have been. In 1739 he referred to his daughter Sally as being ill and although she recovered this may have left her delicate. In 1741 when Dr Clegg, Sally and her sister Betty had all been suffering from a malarial fever for some weeks he recorded with great grief that Sally died on July 14th, aged only twenty-three. He wrote sadly:

'She was the most pious and dutiful child I ever had, and this is the greatest breach that was ever made upon my earthly comforts. She was a most dutiful and affectionate daughter to me . . .'

Six months later at the end of January 1742 his wife died quite suddenly and on January 30th Clegg wrote in his diary:

'This is the widest breach that was ever made upon me. The greatest loss I ever sustained. I am now deprived of a most pious, prudent, diligent, careful and affectionate companion.'

Throughout 1742 and 1743 his remaining unmarried daughter, Betty, kept house for him and he continued as busy as ever with his extensive practice, his parish work, his farming and his social round. Then in 1744 she decided to marry. He recorded:

'July 25th. Walked up to Chappel to peruse a settlement deed on behalf of my daughter, who intends shortly to be married to Thos Middleton, grandson to Mr. Robt, Middleton my old friend.

'July 27th. My daughter was married this morning by Mr. Bardsley at Chappel-en-le-Frith. We all dined at Thos. Middletons, and I returned with my sons about the middle of the afternoon. I am now left in solitary state. Son Benjamin sets out for the Academy at Kendal and then I shall have no child with me. I am therefore advised by my children and friends to look out for a suitable companion.'

He was not long in making up his mind as the entries for August indicate:

'Aug. 16th. Walked up to Chappel, met Mr. Thomas Kyrke and came to a conclusion about marrying. I had been in great perplexity about it, but now resolved to follow ye conduct of Providence and cast all my care upon the ever blessed God.

'Aug. 17th. I was much indisposed and afflicted with what we call ye Hypocondriac passion.

'Aug. 22nd. I set out with my friends to Disley and there was married by Mr. Robinson of Macclesfield to Mrs. Eyre. Mr. Culcheth and Mr. Jones were with us and several other friends.

'Aug. 23rd. I find myselfe now much better both in body and mind; calm, cheeful, composed and easy.'

From further entries in the diary it appears that Mrs Eyre

was the wealthy and attractive widow of a silk manufacturer with a grown-up daughter, who had been rather spoiled. Clegg recorded:

'Jan. 17th 1745. We were invited to dine at Fford and I took my wife with me and Miss Eyre. The latter stayed there all night and the night after. I returned after dinner with my wife, and my man having got too much to drink fell from ye mare and was in great danger of losing his life.

'Jan. 26th. My dear hears bad news from abroad. A ship is taken by ye Ffrench which had 700 pounds worth of silk on board, pertaining to the mill at Stockport. A 12th of the loss lies upon her.'

The Rebellion of 1745 caused great alarm, as the rebel army under Prince Charles advanced southwards. Dr Clegg noted:

'Nov. 25th. We hear ye Rebels are advancing fast towards Manchester and the people are removing and concealing their best effects.

'Nov. 26th. . . . At night I sent away my wife's cloaths and Linen and some writings to be concealed awhile.

'Nov. 27th. We hear some of ye Rebels are come to Manchester. Our town is full of Refugees.

'Dec. 5th. We heard all the Rebels were in Derby . . .

'Dec. 10th. Ye Rebels have all returned to Manchester. They took several persons with them from Stockport. Blessed be God, ye silk mill is safe.

'Jan. 9th. . . . This day I sent my son John in Manchester an horse load of provisions, meal, bacon, cheese and butter, towards making up the loss sustained by the devouring Rebels.'

Apart from a further note in February somewhat prematurely reporting the dispersal of the rebels two months prior to Culloden there is no other mention of the Rebellion. There is, however a very business-like entry regarding his arrangements with his wife:

'March 28th. I settled accounts with my wife, and she paid

me what I had laid out for her, and for one years board for her daughter and grandson. In all it amounted to £34 18s.'

Despite this business-like accounting he appears to have enjoyed four years of very happy married life with his second wife. In August of 1748 he recorded an outing with her that nearly ended in an accident:

'Augst 4th. Carried my wife to Chinley Head, only for a ride out, for we never alighted, but we narrowly escaped a fall from the mare. Something in ye saddle or pillion hurt her and she kicked; my wife came off, but blessed be God had no hurt.'

This was, however, one of his last outings with his wife, for in November she fell ill and after five days died; he wrote brokenly:

'Nov. 24th. Thus the wise, the just and the good God has seen fitt to deprive me of an excellent woman, a pleasant companion, and a most affectionate woman, and I am left in my advanced age in a solitary state.

'Dec. 6th. My heart is heavy and at times full of sorrow for the great loss of my dear wife. I . . . cannot yet conquer grief. When I recollect ye agreeableness of her person, the beauties that even in her advanced age adorned her body and mind; when I reflect on her good sense and judgement, her great prudence and discretion, ye cheerfulness of her temper and conversation, and her most affectionate concern for my health and ease and satisfaction, it fills me with sorrow that I cannot express and scarce know how to bear.'

In January of 1749 he had the satisfaction of hearing his son, Benjamin, who was preparing for the ministry, preach. His entry read:

'Jan. 8th. We had a flood in the morning. Son Benjamin preached. I hear the Methodists were offended with his discourse. He insisted so much on the necessity of a good life in order to achieve Salvation by Christ.'

Life with his stepdaughter Miss Eyre, however, was not

proving easy. He noted:

'March 7th. Some harsh language that passed between me and Ms Eyre gave me great uneasiness after.'

He took steps to pacify her by making over all his late wife's estate to her children and in May was clearly delighted to record further good news of his son Benjamin.

'May 26th. Son Benjamin tells me he is called to be a Minister at Mansfield, and has accepted the call . . . What a seasonable provision has God made for him. For ever blessed be God for all his goodness to me and mine.'

In April of the following year, 1750, he set out for Derby to his son Benjamin's ordination, along with his grand-daughter Nancy Clegg and his stepdaughter Miss Ann Eyre. He entered it thus:

'April 10th. We reached Derby about noon and dined at the George Inn; Son Benjamin came to us from Notting-ham.

'April 11th. We went to ye Meeting Place about 11. Ordained four ministers with the usual ceremonies, including son Benjamin. We saw at Derby a Rhinoceros and live Crocodile.'

He continued with much the same round of work in his parish and his practice, but still managed to find time for diversions on occasions:

'Oct. 1st. R. Oldham dined with us and we walked up to Chappel and diverted ourselves at shuffle-board, and spent ye rest of ye day at Mr. Walker's.'

An indication of the extent of his influence in the district as well as a sidelight on electioneering in 1751 appeared in the diary:

'June 13th. A new election we hear is coming on for a member to succeed ye Marquess of Huntington, who is called up to the House of Lords. The Duke of Devonshire sets up his 3rd son, the Lord Frederick Cavendish, for a Knight of the Shire.

'June 14th. Mr. Bagshaw came over with a letter from his

Grace. Mr. Ash the parson of the Forest came to us and we consulted how to secure votes; and I rid out to Bowden Head to secure some there.

'June 25th. Mr. Bagshaw brought me 10 pounds from the D. of Devonshire.'

His son Joseph, though still in London, seems to have been doing well and had not forgotten him for there are occasional entries such as:

'Oct. 19th. Last night I received from Joseph a barrel of oysters and a pott of British Herrings, an acceptable present.'

Throughout the severest weather and despite some nasty falls from his horse, he continued his medical practice. On 1st April 1752 he recorded a further hazard:

'After dinner I was called to John Barns, his wife just delivered of a dead child and in great danger. Thence I was called to a daughter of Will. Grant our Clark. Thence I rid up to Slack Hall and down to Fford, where I staid too late. I found the rum and water I drank disordered my head when I came out into the cold air, for there was a very cold East wind. I must be more careful to avoid excess for ye future, but I came safe home, blessed be God.'

Nor did he spare himself in his parochial duties, but he also noted uneasily:

'April 12th. I preached both parts of the day from Gal.C.8. and was much spent at night, and so low spirited as to be scarcely able to perform the duties of our family worship. The Congregation was but thin, tho' the weather was good, which gave me some uneasiness.'

On July 8th another source of uneasiness appeared:

'. . . At night Buxton, a tanner at Wirksworth, who makes courtship to Ms Eyre, came to me and stayed all night, and by ye entertainments she gave him I concluded she shortly intends to marry him, and leave me solitary, which gives me great uneasiness.

'July 9th. Buxton continued with Ms Eyre all day.'

In practice he had never got on well with his stepdaughter and he resolved not to oppose the marriage. The following year, 1753, he recorded baldly:

'April 2nd. Ms Eyre set out for Marple this morning to be married to S. Buxton some day this week.'

His ultimate solution to obtaining a replacement for her was simple enough as he noted:

'May 4th. I took a ride to Cats Tor about an Housekeeper that was offered me; I went to let them know that I had at present no occasion for any; having determined to make a trial of my grand daughter.'

He seems to have managed to live very happily with his granddaughter Nancy once his stepdaughter was away and his remarks about the latter come as near to expressing dislike as he was capable of doing:

'May 9th. S. Buxton came for his wife and brought his partner with him. They all dined and drank tea; and then sett off; and very glad I am that she is gone and that we are parted in peace. Now I hope for peace at home.'

In December of the same year, 1753, he recorded his principal remaining anxiety and his delightfully simple solution.

'Dec. 4th. I was under an apprehension of dying shortly and my greatest concern was for ye continuation of ye means of Salvation in these parts after my Decease, but God can provide, and on him I rely. With a view to this I have a Ticket purchased for me in the Irish Lottery. If Providence shall favour me with a Prize, I have determined that one halfe of it shall be applied for that use or to some other that shall appear more pious and charitable.'

Sad to relate providence did not provide such an easy solution, nor on the other hand did he die as soon as he had expected. Although well on in years he continued his practice and his ministry to the end. In 1755 there is the entry:

'Febry. 19th. At night I receiv'd a parcel of Bibles, New

Testaments and other good books from Mr. Chandler of London, given by the Society for promoting Christian knowledge among the poor. I am thankful to God for them and hope many others will have greater reason to be so too.'

Finally came the entry: 'July 29th 1755 . . .' and nothing more, for after a short illness Dr James Clegg died on August 5th aged seventy-six. There can be no doubt that he left a warm feeling of affection and admiration behind him in the Chapel-en-le-Frith area. Something of the same feeling must be experienced by anyone after reading his very human account of his life.

## NOTES

1 Chapel-en-le-Frith. Usually so abbreviated in local speech.
2 Ran away from.
3 Anger.

# 4

## The Rev. Seth Ellis Stevenson

### Schoolmaster and Pluralist: Nottinghamshire

*Fill'd three Vessels with Ruisin Wine*

For proof that Dr James Clegg was an exceptional country divine in the eighteenth or any other century, it is only necessary to glance at the rather scanter diary entries of a contemporary, not so far east of him in neighbouring Nottinghamshire. The Rev. Seth Ellis Stevenson (1724-1783) was aged twenty-eight when his diary opens in 1752. Married in 1750, he had one son, William, born in 1751. Unfortunately only fragments of what was almost certainly a lifetime's record remain, covering the years 1752 to 1755, and they provide only sparse information as to the man himself. Enough is available, however, to form an idea of his tastes and character and to make his principal interests and way of life clear.

Quite apart from being an Anglican priest rather than a Presbyterian minister, the Rev. Seth Ellis Stevenson, headmaster of Retford Grammar School during one of the worst periods in its history, holder of two livings, rector of Treswell and vicar of Waddingsworth, was a very different character from Clegg. Stevenson was a determined horticulturalist and farmer, more concerned with these incidentals than with his duties either as a schoolmaster or priest. A brewer of remarkable quantities of ale and a winemaker on almost as large a scale, he seems to have been far more occupied with

*The church at Treswell, near Retford, still surrounded by farming land, where the Rev. Seth Ellis Stevenson was pluralist rector in the mid-eighteenth century.*

his farm, his garden, and his still-room or brewhouse than with his parishioners. His own affairs and his creature comforts took first priority.

The first three entries in January are typical of his various activities:

'Jan. 18. The Quarter Hhd[1] was drawn out, having been on the Tap since 28th Decr. last. Tapp'd a 24 gallon Vessel same day.

'20th. Bot a Cow & Calf of Thos Clareboro' for £4, the Cow 4½ years of her third calf. Wind S.S.E. boisterous with much Rain & a Thaw.

'21st. Lent Jno Colton 2s for a Week.'

Small-scale usury was one of Seth Ellis Stevenson's minor sidelines. What, if any, rate of interest he charged is hard to say since his diary and his Account Book supplemented each other in a somewhat confusing manner, in each instance compounding confusion.

It was perhaps typical of the man that although his winnings at cards, which he played regularly, were almost always noted in his diary, his rather more frequent losses were recorded only in his Account Book.

Two early entries in February illustrate this point:

'5th. Dr. Raines[2] owes 1s 6d won at Cards.

'14th. Won 6s at Cards.'

In view of a subsequent entry in June it is perhaps significant that the entries for the entire month of March are missing, having apparently been torn out of the diary. A series of very typical entries for May and June give the flavour of his life:

'May 6. Tapp'd a Qr Cask of the New Ale — the last ½ Hhd having lasted since 24 March.

'7th. Black heifer took Bull.

'12th. Grey Cow calved a Bull Calf.

'June 18. Lent Tom Bedford 1s — he owed 6d before. Planted near 440 Savoys betwixt the Beans in ye Lower Moorgate Close.'

So far very typical of this farming and gardening divine;
then, unexpectedly, comes the entry:

'23. (Sunday ye 21 — Seth Ellis Stevenson died, betwixt
10 & 11 o'clock in ye Morng after abt. 8 Hours Indispositn.
agd 13 Weeks.)'

Here it seems is the explanation of the torn-out pages in
March, which almost certainly recorded the birth and
probably the christening of his second son. The entry of the
death it may be noted was on the 23rd, presumably the day
of the funeral, although no mention of it was made. There
must have been a great deal of family anxiety, grief and
mourning, which can only be guessed at, concealed behind
this brief Roman Father's record of his son's death.

The next entry in June is a typical farming note regarding
haymaking, followed by two more in July.

'29. Cutt Moorgate Top Close. Mowing (being very
difficult) 3s 6d and 8½d Beer.'

Since mowing was so difficult it is a reasonable assumption that it was a laid field of hay and hence not a very good
crop. This is borne out by the entry for the 5th of July, which
recorded:

'July 5. Bot 4 loads of Hay of Jno Cole, to be laid down
for 25s per Load. Good Loads & dry hard Hay.'

This in turn is followed by the entry:

'6. Remov'd the Cows into Bottom Grounds. Flock't Cow
suppos'd to have taken Bull there. Sarah[3] for her Saucy
Behaviour turn'd away.'

Quite incidentally in his next entry, along with his haymaking records, he slips in his first mention of his duties as a
priest:

'July 9. Put Moor gate Close Hay into Pike. Jno Hobson
employ'd abt 1½ Hour — Stubbing did the rest. To preach
on Sunday next at Headon (M) & at Eaton in the Eveng.'

In August a gardening entry gives some idea of the scope
of his activities:

'Aug 8. Cutt up the Strawberries & earth'd 'em. Weed &

clean'd the Allies. Earth'd up the first Crops of Cellery for good & the 2nd Crop the first time. Sew 2 Rows of Burdock Spinage in the corner Garden and set out 12 Savoy Plants near them. Quills 170 — 7½d.'[4]

The 'Quills', then used, of course, for pens, were very cheap at this price and since he made his own ink, as well, the costs of writing up his diary were not great. In many ways, indeed, he was nearly self-sufficient. As for instance:

'Aug. 10. Drew off the Raisin Wine into 53 Qurt Bottles.'

An interesting entry followed soon afterwards:

'Sept. 2. N.B. Thursday, wch wod have been ye 3d of September is by a late Act of Parliament made ye 14th — Eleven whole Days being here sunk & annihilated.'[5]

The year 1752 ended with two entries:

'Dec. 23. Tapp'd the first Vessel of the last Brewg.

'31. Sacramt at Treswell. 33 Communicts . . .'

The year 1753 opened with a very typical entry:

'Jan 1st. Balanc'd with Uncle Rose & recd all but for the Cheese wch is to be pd in kind. Gave Eliz. Neaves warng to leave her house.'

He seems to have acted as a distributing centre for monthly and annual magazines, no doubt making a small charge for his services. His entry for 22nd January read:

'Set Sandwich Beans under Mr. Mason's Wall.

'Memdm. Mr Robinson takes in no more of the Magaz. than the Sup [Supplement] for 1752. Mr Holliday discontinues them. Mr Tomlinson discontinues them & also the Review & takes only Rapin's Continuation. Mr. Bingham discontinues ye N. Universal Magaz. N.B. he has paid me from the Beging, Supplemt included. The first Advertisement in ye Stamford paper was Thursday 18th January 1753.'

Two personal entries in February stand out in relief amongst the monotony of the farming and gardening notes:

'Feb 11. Lost my Watch (on Treswell Bank) in going to Burton — & had the good fortune to find it agn after missing it 4 hours. Charles Silkston assisted in ye Search I gave him 2s 6d. Mrs Turner paid 1s for 1lb of Mustard.

'19th Mary Hobson stole Beef out of my Pantry — wch Fact — to avoid a Prosecution — she confess'd & beg'd Pardon. No further Service for her or her Husband.'

Bearing in mind that any theft to the value of 40s. and over was still a capital offence this latter entry takes on considerable significance. Remembering also the entry on the death of his son, it is possible to evaluate the domestic drama concealed behind this terse entry about the wretched couple John and Mary Hobson. Although Mary Hobson escaped the gallows, or transportation, she and her husband did not escape due punishment. Stevenson was not of a forgiving nature. He noted:

'30th February. Gave Jno Hobson Notice — before Isaac Goodlad — to leave my House next Lammas.'[6]

Nor was he one to miss an opportunity to make a profit whenever possible. Another result of this upheaval was noted in July:

'July 14. Benjn Beardsell took the Tenent late Hobson's — to have the Privilege of laying Wood &c under the Cow-place Hovel, & the Swine-Coat, provided yt when he has not a Pig, I may have ye Use of it. — to enter at Lammas. O.S. At £3 per Ann. And to leave the Windows &c in as Good Condition as he finds ym. The rent at equal Paymts half Yearly.'

In his Accounts, kept separately, for the same date is an entry:

'A new dark brown Wig 15s.'

His permanent gardener-handyman, Duke Allan, figures fairly frequently in the diary, somewhat understandably in view of his great interest in gardening. The above entry on the wig is followed finally by another:

'Sept. 21. Gave Duke Allan an Old Wigg.'

The employment of other servants is noted in an entry in October, which read:

'21. Eliz. Rainer came — at 55s Wage. Benj. Wethering-
ham came at 30s pr Annm. I promise to teach him
(occasionally) Writing & Accts & to give him now & then
some of my old Cloathes.'

A further entry in December showed that he allowed few
opportunities for profit-making to escape him.

'Dec. 3. Lett the 2 Low Rooms & 2 Chambers only, in the
Back Tenemt at 38s per Ann. Rent ½ Yearly to Theodosia
Fluring. Enter at Candlemas next — We to have free Access
to ye Garrets — She to leave the Windows &c in perfect
Repair.'

A later entry in December was an early example of its
kind:

'16. Recd. 2s for a Wedding at Treswell by Banns.'[7]

Two other entries in December coupled together read:

'10th. Saml Twelves came a Liking.[8]

'21. Hir'd Saml Twelves at 45s a Year, commencing 10th
Inst. and at the Expiratn of the year Each of Us to give the
other a Qrs warning if we shd not agree.'

Early in 1754 the scale of his gardening activities is
revealed in a typical entry, dated 4th January:

'Put all the rest of my blowing Tulip[9] Roots into the Right
Hand Border — mounting to 460 & 369 Ranunculas — Mr
Swift's Ranunculas beginn at the Bottom & run abt 2/3 of 1
Line next to the Gravel Walk.'

On the 6th of January he entertained company and
noted:

'Messrs. Mosman, Bragg, Jno & Stow Wade, Ward,
Hudson, Haworth & Hutchinson & Morton to Supper.'[10]

Three entries closely following one another indicate that
he did sometimes attend to his duties as rector and schoolmaster:

'Jan. 30. Walked to Treswell — did Duty.

'Feb. 3. Preach'd at Carlton and 9th Time & at Elksley the
3rd Time — for Mr. Parker.

'Feb. 4. Balanc'd with Mr. Morton[11] — pd him £3.15s

taking only 10s as Entrance Fee for his Sons . . .'

A significant event in the life of his son William, aged three, was entered:

'March 7. Put Billey into Breeches.'[12]

An equally brief and laconic entry marked his own birthday:

'14th. Birthday — 30 Years.'

A very typical instance of his conflict of interests followed:

'17. Preach'd in the Morng at Elksley — & read Prayers in ye Eveng. 11th Sunday Service for Mr. Barker — exclusive of the Sunday when Mr. Hurst & I exchang'd.

'Grizled Cow calv'd a Bull Calf.

'23. Engag'd to take Care of the Cure of Mattersay for Mr. Waddington (Every Alternate Sunday in the Morng) — for £16 per Ann. He is to take upon him Occasnl. Offices. Commence at Easter.'

The rest of the year is filled with similar entries concerning his farming, gardening, wine or ale-making, but seldom much concerning his rectorial or schoolmastering duties. It is only fair to suggest that it was meant to be read in conjunction with his Account Book and serving as a reminder of details which might otherwise have been overlooked. Thus in November came an entry indicating that the hiring of Samuel Twelves had not been successful:

'25. Saml. Twelves left — & Wm. Stevenson came at 50s per year Wage. I promise to teach him to write as Occasion offers. Kill'd the Pig & it weighed 18 Stone.'

Thus it may be argued that his entry on Christmas Day is more of an accounting than a record of service:

'Decr. 25. Sacramt at Mattersay (25 Communicts) Money then collected 4s 1¾d (Thos Sellers Wife, churchg & Child Xting abt. Midsummer last — at Mattersay, 7d — recd this day.'

A characteristic glimpse of his reading matter is to be had from an entry in late January 1755:

'Jan 30. Sold to Mr Hawksmore the Hist of the Reformatn. I took no more yn 10s 6d for it.'

A much more familiar series of entries followed shortly:

'Feb. 23. Put the Raisins (387lbs wt) to Water. 73 Galls Wine Measure. Added 28 of Fruit more in all 415.

'Mar. 13. Fill'd three Vessels with Raisin Wine, wch ran off from the Fruit with pressing, containing 19, 17 & 14 Galls. Drew off ye Remdr of ye last Yrs Raisin Wine consisting of 78 Bottles.

'15. Put 24 Galls of Water more to the Raisin.'

A laconic entry on 18th April noted:

'Wedding Day — 5 Years Ago.'

It is closely followed by another entry which almost certainly gave Stevenson more cause for rejoicing:

'30. Sold the Grizled Cow to Mr. Sutton Scofton for £8 10s clear Money.'

The school holidays seem to have been in May, for he recorded:

'May 8. Billy White went home for the Holyday.

'10. James & Roger went home.'

This is followed by an entry in July:

'July 15. Nanny Ellis, ½ Years Washg for Roger 9s. due L. day last. ½ Years Do for Jemmy due Midsummer 9s.'

One of the last entries read, typically enough:

'Oct 10. Bottled off the Red Port from Mr. Pearson & there was 100 2 Quts. Good Measure 43 Bottles.'

The final entry, perhaps relating to one of his boarders left behind during the Christmas holiday read:

'25. Wm Tomlinson & Jack digg pottatoes.'

There the fragment of the journal ends abruptly, but enough has been quoted to reveal the character of the man. Tight-fisted and acquisitive, energetic in almost all matters except it seems the Church or the school, (he was for instance a moving spirit in the Chesterfield canal when it was started). His real interests were farming and gardening, wine-making and ale-brewing. His show of tulips and ranunculi in the rectory garden must have been outstanding, but anyone overdue with his rent could expect no mercy. It is only fair to add that the diary undoubtedly portrays the businessman rather than the priest, but equally clearly the former dominated the latter. He might have been able to reach the minds of his neighbouring farmers when he preached, but there can be little doubt that Ralph Josselin was a better priest, if not necessarily a better farmer.

## NOTES

1 Hogshead, approximately 18½ gallons.
2 The family physician.
3 It may be presumed that Sarah was a maidservant who had been arbitrarily sent packing and not one of the herd of cows.
4 In these parts quills were generally obtained by the cruel practice of plucking the geese alive annually.
5 The Reform of the Julian Calendar, introduced by Pope Gregory III in 1582 was only adopted by Great Britain in 1752 when eleven days were dropped to bring it into line with the new form by an Act of Parliament, which was bitterly opposed by many clergymen and most farmers.
6 1st of August.
7 About this time an Act of Parliament was passed whereby the old method by which couples could be married with no other formality than presenting themselves and paying the parson's fees was replaced with the publishing of banns on three consecutive Sundays and the consent of parents in the case of minors. This was aimed at heiress hunters and the notorious Fleet parsons.
8 An evocative term meaning on probation as a servant.
9 Tulips were a mid-eighteenth century passion, recently introduced from Holland.
10 The guests consisting of his farmer neighbours, his maltster, his brewer and his grocer, were perhaps indicative of his principal interests.
11 His maltster.
12 It was, of course, the fashion then for all children in the nursery to wear dresses until it was decided the boys were old enough to be breeched. The changeover was regarded as a significant point in their lives, varying from three years of age to as late as six. William Stevenson, then aged three, was to be proprietor of the Norfolk *Mercury* for thirty-five years and died in Norwich in 1821.

# 5

## The Rev. George Ridpath

### Border Minister and Historian: Roxburghshire

*Came home about 9, and slept on Voltaire*

George Ridpath (1717-1772) was minister of Stitchel (or Stitchill) three miles north of Kelso in Roxburghshire from 1742 until his death. His father, after whom he was named as the eldest son, was minister of nearby Ladykirk in Berwickshire from 1712 to 1740. Brought up in the manse and educated at Edinburgh University, Ridpath was a distinguished classical scholar and linguist, able to read in Greek, Latin, Hebrew, French and Italian.

Although theology was conspicuously absent from his very wide range of reading, he was a conscientious minister, assiduously visiting the aged and sick in his parish and often prescribing simple remedies. His glebe farm, his garden, the circulating library in Kelso and his social round kept him otherwise busily engaged. Apart from occasional visits to Edinburgh, mostly to attend the General Assembly, he rarely travelled more than ten or fifteen miles from his parish, yet he clearly led a full and enjoyable life.

A bachelor when the diary was written, his mother and sister Nancy lived with him and kept house for him. Amongst his neighbours and close friends was the Rev. George Turnbull of nearby Sprouston, son of the Rev. George Turnbull of Tyninghame. The diary, two manu-

*A pastoral view of the Eildon Hills from the east of the kirk and manse at Stitchill, which the Rev. George Ridpath would have recognised. Only the cattle and afforestation have altered since the mid-eighteenth century.*

script volumes of daily entries, begins in April 1755:

'Sunday Aprile 13th. Wind westerly, pretty high. Lectured on Psalm 68 v 22. Preached on 1 Cor 15 vv 56 and 57.'

Two consecutive entries later in April and four more in May give a clear picture of his interests and activities:

'Friday, Aprile 25th. At Fallsidehill and Home baptising and seeing sick. Robert Turnbull, Mr. Lundy [Minister of Kelso] and Robert's nephew, Hay, who came a day or two ago from Edinburgh to see his uncle, drank tea. Looked at night at some things in Mead's *Monita et Praecepta Medica*. [Published in 1751 by Dr Richard Mead.]

'Munday, Aprile 28th. Saw sick in town a.m. and then went to Kelso to attend the Culloden Club; thirteen of us only there, a variety of accidents hindering the attendance of members. Had a song, the making of which amused me part of last week, but could scarce get it sung for want of performers. Rode home with Sir Robert [Sir Robert Pringle, 3rd Baronet of Stitchel, Ridpath's principal heritor] betwixt 7 & 8.

'Thursday, May 8th. Spent the forenoon in new cocking my hat, shaving etc. Robert Turnbull came and dined. Set out along with him for Greenlaw, when Mr. Dysart [Matthew Dysart, minister of Eccles] also came. Staid there all night. D. Hume's *History*, which John Hume [Minister of Greenlaw] has been reading the principal subject of discourse.

'Friday, May 9th. Set out in the morning with John and his two sons for Abbey [St. Bathans]. Had a pleasant ride and got there about ten. A considerable congregation, and the sermon without, which agreed ill with my toothache. Sate till near 6, drank rather too long and were too noisy. Some girls there that were animating; especially Walter Hart's daughter. . . . Had a good plain dinner. Rode to Polwarth in the evening, along with Robert Turnbull, Matt. Dysart and Cupples [Minister of Swinton] . . .

'Saturday, May 10th. Set out from Polwarth along with Mr. Dysart. Robert and I dined and drank tea at Eccles. Came home about six. Saw Edward Dodd's wife who has seemed a-dying these ten days; and did something for tomorrow . . .

'Munday, May 12th. A.m. at Home seeing sick. P.m. went to Sir Robert's, who has been ailing and is looking but indifferently. Came home about 9. and slept on Voltaire.'

On the 27th of May he went to Edinburgh to attend the General Assembly. He recorded:

'On Munday morning set out along with Mr. Lundy . . . Lodged in the Solicitor's [Andrew Pringle, Solicitor General] along with John Home [minister of Athelstaneford] . . .'

He noted his feelings regarding his stay in Edinburgh very humanly on his return home:

'At Edinburgh not unhappy on the whole; yet not so happy as I might have been. Could not use perfect freedom in my quarters, the Solicitor's, where I was under some sort of necessity of lodging, he having been here himself to ask me. Yet this was wholly owing to my shyness, for by him I was treated with great civility. John Home's flow of wit and spirits, much encouraged by the company of the Great, to which he has had more familiar access than almost any of his profession, threw a sort of damp on me. Clothes and equipments were not so good as the taste of the age and a town life requires. The room where I lodged was gloomy and extremely ill aired, and sometimes my living was too high, though this I bore very well. To live agreeably in Edinburgh I find it would be necessary for me to live in a Lodging, where I would be at perfect liberty; to be well equipped in point of dress; and to associate more with people of speculation and learning than those of a gayer turn; yet not altogether to avoid the latter. But the greatest disadvantage of all for that sort of life is my want of facility in making up to strangers and conversing with them. A disadvantage partly from complexion, but chiefly from education and my ordinary train of life, that I believe I shall never wholly get over.'

Like the Rev. Seth Ellis Stevenson his farming and gardening kept him fully occupied at times as he recorded:

'Saturday, October 11th. Prepared for tomorrow and read out the Reviews and Magazines. Got all my corn led in, and the hay-stack right built, which we were hindered from doing on Wednesday by night coming on. John Miller and Mr. Dawson called p.m. on their way to a dance at Sir Robert's.

'Friday, October 17th. Planted my tulips and ranunculuses, tho' the ground is rather too wet yet; did not care to delay it any longer.'

In April of 1756 Ridpath became embroiled, along with his great friend James Allan, minister of Eyemouth, in a long and worrying series of negotiations on behalf of his younger brother Philip. He had been a schoolmaster in Berwick, but was in the process of being presented to the ministry at Hutton at the instigation of Lord Marchmont. The first entry of many on the subject read:

'Monday, Aprile 19th. Saw sick in the town a.m. and was at Home p.m. Married also there Alexander Richardson. Got a letter from Philip in the morning, informing me that Lord Marchmont had wrote to Lady Hilton informing her that Philip's Presentation had been stopt at the Secretary's office, by the Duke of Argyle, Lord Home having informed him that my Lord Marchmont had procured it in opposition to the inclination of the principal gentlemen of the parish, particularly Mr. Renton. On this Lord Marchmont desires Lady Hilton to try to procure Mr. Renton's concurrence, a thing I suppose she would never attempt as the attempt would be altogether vain. James Allan has been sent for to Hutton-hall to consult with on this occasion and Hilton wrote to Marchmont on Friday evening, insisting I suppose on Marchmont's making a point of obtaining the Presentation for Philip; the success of which however, looks a little uncertain when there is so formidable an opposition.'

The affair was complicated by a rivalry between Lord Marchmont and Lord Home, the latter claiming the right of presentation of both Stitchel and Hutton. Ridpath thus found himself in the invidious position of opposing on his brother's behalf the man he regarded as both friend and benefactor. It involved endless litigation up to the House of Lords and references to it appear continually in the diary entries. In October Ridpath and James Allan went to Borthwick in order to have an opportunity of discussing the matter with the Lord Advocate, Robert Dundas, in nearby Arniston. The entry read:

'Sunday, October 17th. I lectured on 16th Psalm fluently enough. James Allan preached. Lord Advocate and family in the Kirk. We went over to Arniston to dine with him and before dinner talked over our affair . . . Arniston is a very beautiful place, but we had no time to see much of it . . .'

His youngest brother, William, was also preparing for the ministry and was eventually to become minister of Edrom. In August 1757 Ridpath recorded:

'Tuesday, August 2nd. Went to the Presbytery, where Will delivered his exercise and addition. His voice and accent much better than I had expected, but too many blunders and hesitations. Drank tea in Dobby's and had a library meeting where only 6 were present. Commissioned however two or three books.'

This referred to the Kelso circulating library of which Ridpath and Turnbull were among the moving spirits. It was through this that he very quickly obtained so many of the books be recorded reading soon after their publication. One of the earliest libraries of its kind in Scotland, maintained by the subscriptions of members, he benefited greatly from it, even if he spent quite a lot of time in its management.

An entry in October recorded Will's progress:

'Tuesday, October 4th. At the Presbytery, where Will delivered the last of his tryals, and was licensed. He acquitted himself, on the whole, very tolerably. Drank some punch at Wood's with Messrs. Turnbulls and came home betwixt 7 and 8. Read last night's Edinburgh papers. Journalised and looked to a sermon for Kelso tomorrow.'

An entry on Saturday October 8th reveals how his life was bounded by the confines of his parish; he noted:

'. . . Never was in Teviotdale before farther than Jedburgh. The ride from Mount Teviot to Hawick is a very pleasant one. A fine country of corn fields and gently rising green hills on both sides of the Teviot with some well situated gentlemen's seats and villages. I have not seen so fine a strath . . . Hawick, itself, is a prettily situated town, with its waters, bridges, gardens and green hills around it . . .'

In October of the following year, 1758, he was forced to approach Lord Marchmont on his brother's behalf over an appeal to the House of Lords. He wrote:

'Thursday, October 16th. . . . I set out for Greenlaw upon an appointment there with John Hume and Matthew Dysart to see Lord Marchmont. We were very lucky in finding nobody there but My Lord. . . . My Lord soon introduced the Hutton business and gave me the opportunity of putting into his hands the information which I had carried along with me and which he had not seen before. . . . He was so good as to challenge me at coming away, for this being only the second time of my having seen him. The true reason for which, besides the aversion I have to be dangling on the great, was chiefly a scruple at making court to a rival and adversary of Lord Home, to whom I have been so much obliged and whose interest I could scarce be justified in opposing were it not in a case where the interest of a brother is so fundamentally concerned . . .'

In February and March 1759 there were two contrasting entries each of which, in their own way, were very revealing:

'Tuesday, February 27th. Read the newspapers, from

which I did not learn much. Wrought a little in the garden and gave some attendance to a brewing of strong ale . . .

'Friday, March 2nd. Shaved a.m. and rode to Eccles, where I dined and drank tea. At night I looked to some things in an Italian Grammar: 'tis long since I read anything in that language, but I must not forget it.'

Later in March came the final decision on the 'troublesome affair'.

'Wednesday, March 14th. . . . Found a letter here when I came home from Philip . . . informing me that . . . the cause of Hutton was decided by the Peers on the 7th, and given for the Crown without any difficulty. . . . And so this troublesome affair is at last come to the end we desired, for which we have ground to be thankful to the Supreme Disposer.'

An accounting a day later revealed what had been involved:

'Friday, March 16th. Wrote Philip. Calculated the amount of the expense of my Edinburgh journeys about his cause. The eight journeys come to about £6 13s, which considering that I was once ten days in the town, and sometimes paid both for James Allan and myself, is certainly a very moderate sum. . . . At night read the Life of Drummond of Hawthornden.'

The last act in the drama took place quietly and successfully:

'Thursday, May 3rd. . . . Philip's Ordination Day. Cupples preached an excellent sermon ad clerum, and his charge was very good. The dinner consisted of solids, very good and in good order [It had been prepared by his sisters.] between 40 and 50 better sort of people were dined and a . greater number of inferiors. . . . All sorts of people seemed to be extremely happy . . .'

Ridpath's comment on his brother's performance in the pulpit was the height of praise for a reserved Border Scot. He noted:

'Sunday, May 6th. Somewhat windy from W. to N. Rode over in the evening from Eyemouth to Hutton, where I preached a.m. on John 8.32. Philip preached p.m. and baptised a child. Got through his work well enough . . .'

In June Ridpath attended the Assembly in Edinburgh once again and recorded:

'Munday, June 4th. The Assembly rose; scarce ever had an Assembly less business or was more infrequently convened. The Commissioner inclined strongly that it should have been finished on Friday or Saturday, but the spirit of the majority was so much against it that he gave way. This being the Prince of Wales' birthday, the company with whom I dined dealt pretty liberally in Bonum Magnums after dinner and meeting afterwards sate pretty late. Reckonings amount to 7s 6d, a very extravagant sum, and which I scarce should have been led into had I not been making a sort of court to Carlisle who undertook very readily to put a Memorial into Baron Grant's hands relating to the vacant stipend at Hutton.

'Tuesday, June 5th. The Commission met a.m. and heard a Cause from the Synod of Glenelg. Aeneas Sage contra Aeneas M'Aulay, a charge of heresy for a sermon containing a strange jumble of Hutchesonian and Moravian nonsense. After a pretty long debate the Glenelg sentence was by a great majority in a vote, confirmed, dismissing the latter Aeneas with an admonition and the former with a rebuke for his malignant heresy hunting disposition. Dined at Nicholson's and made several calls. Attended also the burial of poor John Miller, who died on Sunday night.

'Wednesday, June 6th. Rode out with Minna Dawson en croupe, [i.e. riding pillion] who had been a fortnight in town with her cousins. . . . A little fatigued, but more with the circumstances of my town life than with my journey. . . . My getting into company which I was fond of overcame my maxims of frugality, and made me spend more than I should have done, though the whole amount of my ten days' expense was only about two guineas . . .'

Ridpath must often have been involved in heavy drinking bouts, the fashion of the day, as for instance at meetings of the Culloden Club. He often admitted to sitting up late and drinking much, but with one exception never referred to anyone actually being drunk. It may be inferred that he did not like the Rev. Mr Tod, who had succeeded to his father's ministry at Ladykirk for he referred to him in blighting terms:

'Thursday, September 27th. Abraham Ker and Sprot breakfasted here; and we set out before 8. Got to Edrom betwixt 10 and 11. Much company there; 17 Ministers, besides those of the Presbytery. . . . None of our Berwick friends, but Mr. Waite [his brother-in-law] and my sister. . . . Tod was very short in his work, but sate so long after that he got himself very drunk, which, though an unlucky sort of incident, fell better on him than it could have done on anybody else. Far the greatest part of the company went away early in the afternoon; and tho' there was some noise and merriment, yet there is no appearance of excess, but in Tod . . .'

In October he heard of the impending marriage of Miss Madeleine Pringle, daughter of Sir Robert, to Sir John Hall of Dunglass. He wrote:

'Friday, October 12th. Tweed is flooded. Read some in the magazines and some *Architecture*. Was also east the town p.m. seeing sick. Fr. [Frank] Pringle came to drink tea and brought with him a piece of intelligence that rejoiced me extremely. There is a purpose of marriage post in the point of executing betwixt Sir John Hall and Miss Maddy. Frank showed me a testimonial of a Proclamation from Auldhamstocks dated last Sunday, and the Proclamation is to be made here Sunday next. Maddy's *faux pas* at Dunglass has been a very fortunate one, tho' nobody that knows her will think Sir John less fortunate than she. Was so much amused and pleased with this affair, that I did little else than rave about it all evening . . .'

From mention of a *faux pas* it would seem that Miss
Pringle had somehow been compromised and the marriage
was the result. For the next few days Ridpath was ill with a
heavy cold caused he thought 'by sitting at a fire something
too hot among airing clothes'. Then he noted:

'Tuesday, October 16th. In the evening betixt 7 and 8
o'clock had a very unexpected call by a letter from Mr.
Pringle to marry Sir John Hall and his bride. Had kept the
house these two days past and was so much better as not to
be afraid to venture out. Got up about 9 and performed the
ceremony very briefly. Nancy and Minna Dawson had gone
up in the evening and were detained and we three with Sir
John and the family were all the company. Soberly and very
joyous; but never was a simpler affair. Sir John not having
been expected till to-morrow night and having no clothes
but what he rode with, and the bride in her household dress.
Came home with Minna and Nancy after 11.'

The following day he recorded:

'Wednesday, October 17th. Saw a sick woman in the
forenoon. Were invited to Sir Robert's to dine, where was
just the same company as last night. The marriage having
been made a night sooner than was designed none of the
friends cast up. W. Stevenson was to have been there, but
had gone to Wooler Fair. Had a good deal of chat with Sir
John, chiefly about his travels. He has very considerable
funds and is a man of much simplicity and candor. I dare say
Maddy will pass her time with him very comfortably. Came
home in the evening.'

It was the custom of the time for the minister to be
presented by the bride or bridegroom with a pair of gloves or
a hat. On the Saturday after the wedding Ridpath wrote: 'It
is droll that the bride or bridegroom have sent no gloves.' He
was, however, in due course to receive a handsome present
of both gloves and hat. Meanwhile he noted:

'Sunday, October 21st. Sir John Hall and his bride in the
Kirk, with a great train of relations, splendidly drest and

carried in 4 wheel machines. [Four-wheeled carriages were still at this time uncommon in Scotland.] Waited for them by desire. They came about 12 and were dismist before 2.'

On the 13th of November his brother Philip wrote informing him that his niece, the eight-year-old Nancy Waite, and her brother Will, were seriously ill with fever. He wrote:

'Tuesday, November 13th — Wednesday, November 28th. Set out on the Tuesday in less than 2 hours after the letter came to my hand and got to Berwick betwixt 5 and 6 o'clock. By this time the poor child had all the fatal symptoms and was indeed little better than in the agonies of death . . .

'I performed all the duty to her I could, by sitting up all the night by her, and from time to time administering to her some little draughts, part of which she with great efforts got over, till within a few hours of her death; She knew me and looked on me often with pleasure; attempted also to speak to me, but could not articulate her words. Thus it pleased God to remove a great ornament and comfort to her parents and all our family. . . . His will be done . . .

'This scene of distress was scarce over when we learned that the poor boy had had feverish symptoms the preceding night, which continued still with him, tho' gently in the morning. The Doctor took a sufficient quantity of blood from him; and as grief . . . a sore throat and other distressing symptoms . . . the consequence of . . . fatigue in attending poor Nancy rendered my sister incapable of attending the boy I set about this task . . .

'For 6 or 7 nights I lay in a shakedown in the room beside him; and too often had occasion to see how much the ordinary watchers on these occasions stand in need of an Intendant. One night (Sunday Nov 18) I thought him in extreme danger . . . I heard him . . . labouring greatly in his respiration . . . while his two other attendants were fast asleep. . . . I awakened him gently and in that extremity could think of nothing so proper as to give him some pure wine, of which I warmed a teacupfull and sweetened it a little . . . and by the vehement persuasion of a man almost in despair, prevailed with him to swallow a little of it, which . . . gave him so agreeable a relief that without further difficulty he sipped out the whole teacupfull. This revived him. . . . This was the sorest and most distressing night of my attendance, but at the same time, I believe, the most useful . . . and as such strict attendance became unnecessary, I came down to the parlour, where a tent bed had been set up. . . . By this time I was pretty much worn out by anxiety and scarce half of my ordinary sleep for 9 or 10 days. . . . However I got a very good rest the night before I came away. . . . Got a very cold stormy day from N.W to ride home in, and reached home about sunset; having had the good fortune to escape a bitter blast . . .'

He spent some time picking up events on his return and wrote:

'Thursday, November 29th. . . . Mina Dawson dined with us and sate till the evening. She has been with mother and Nancy almost all the time I have been away; which was very good and kind. Nancy has allowed herself to be too much preyed on by anxiety and grief, and is but very so-so in health and spirits.'

On Saturday, December 1st, after, as usual, 'preparing for tomorrow' Ridpath recorded:

'had the comfortable intelligence by a letter from Philip that Willy Waite continues to recover briskly, amuses himself all the day, eats his victuals and takes cheerfully some doses of the bark [quinine] that have been prescribed him.'

Early in 1760 Ridpath visited his sister in Berwick again:

'Wednesday, January 9th. . . . Dinner was just about finished at Mr. Waite's before we reached Berwick. Spent the remainder of the day and the night there. Had some company at tea p.m. Both my sister and Mr. Waite have recovered themselves tolerably from their sore distress and the boy seems to be as hale and vigorous as ever. His being so long from school has given him a turn to play and aversion to his book, which will not be easily overcome.'

About this time the library in Kelso was being moved to new premises and he was deeply involved in supervising this with his friend Robert Turnbull. Throughout the rest of 1760 his life continued with the familiar round of births, deaths and country news, the care of his garden and glebe fields, as well as his regular visits to the sick and elderly, all part of his parish routine, but an interesting sidelight on his character is provided by his comments on his reading in June:

'Thursday, June 19th. Read to the end of Voltaire's *Candide*, a satire on Leibnitz's *System of Optimism* contracting into a small compass in the form of a lively narrative, many of the most horrid scenes of wickedness and misery that are to be met with in the different parts of the world. Tho' it has much of the appearance of [being] graceless and atheistical, yet I am not sure if it contains much more than a just satire on the presumption of Philosophers in pretending to explain or account for particular phenomena of Providence from their systems and partial views. The conclusion of the whole is excellent, travailler sans raisonner, c'est le seul moyen de rendre la vie supportable. Spent all the rest of the day and night in writing letters . . .'

In September he had a small accident with his wife-to-be, which he, significantly, recorded very fully:

'Friday, September 12th. Set out for Fishwick with Mina en croupe. Both, I believe, pleased with our journey, but it had its alloys. Our horse fell with us and we tumbled off a little this side of Swinton Mill. Happilly neither of us hurt, but were obliged to walk forward to the village to get the girth mended. Probably with this toss, a bundle Mina carried amongst her petticoats was loosened and she dropt it somewhere on the road, but did not miss it until we got to Fishwick. Sent immediately a man to see for it, but it was not to be found . . .'

More typical of the daily routine were two December entries:

'Tuesday, December 16th. Saw sick in the town a.m. and made a bargain for a bee-hive. Read London and Edinburgh news. Will came in the evening. Read some more of *Medical Essays* and slept on the life of *Apuleius*.

'Thursday, December 18th. Was at Running-burn seeing a boy ill of the fever, with worms. Wrought a good while in the garden, digging up the root of the old plumb tree, etc Got also the bee-hive brought and set up. Read some more of the London Magazine and slept on Suetonius, a most judicious and entertaining memorialist.'

In 1761 he first noted plans for writing a history of Berwick:

'Friday, March 20th. Much in the garden, where I planted some cabbages and attended the mason repairing the dykes [i.e. dry stone walls] which had several great gaps made in them by the deluge of rain in October last. Read Abercromby, Buchanan, etc. . . .

'Monday, March 23rd. P.m. read historians and began to write from Buchanan and Abercromby the first events relating to Berwick, of which place I have often thought it might be worth while to compile a history, and in particular have had serious thoughts of attempting it.'

In July the diary ended abruptly, but it is pleasing to know that in 1765 at the age of forty-eight he finally married Mina Dawson, daughter of a leading Kelso merchant and friend of the family. During his short married life of seven years they had a son and two daughters, the eldest being six years old when he died in 1772 at the age of fifty-five. It is also pleasant to know that his projected history of Berwick had expanded into a *History of the Borders*, which was published posthumously in 1776 by his younger brother Philip, the minister of Hutton.

# 6

## The Rev. William Cole

### Philosopher and Antiquarian: Buckinghamshire

*Mr. Pomfret sent me an Hare; I return'd him a Goose*

William Cole (1714-1782), fifty-two years old at the start of these diary extracts, was comparatively affluent, with a farm aptly named 'Frog Hall' in the Fens and funds safely invested. He could thus afford to indulge his taste for books and foreign travel within reason. The rector of Blecheley (now Bletchley) in Buckinghamshire and later of Waterbeach in Cambridgeshire, friend and correspondent of Horace Walpole since their schooldays at Eton, M.A. of King's College, Cambridge, Fellow of the Society of Antiquaries, well-travelled, High Tory, in general benevolent, but irascible when crossed, something of a gossip as well as philosopher, he had a keen eye and descriptive turn of phrase. In describing his daily life and his neighbours, Cole also provided an excellent portrait of himself, a portly, elephantine, good-humoured figure.

Only the last eighteen months of his fifteen years at Bletchley and his first six months at Waterbeach are included in these extracts, covering the period from December 1765 to December 1767. These in turn are taken from a folio volume of 469 pages of manuscript amongst a hundred manuscript volumes bequeathed to the British Museum with the provison that they should not be 'inspected or looked at

*Landbeach, alongside the village pound where the Rev. William Cole took the services occasionally.*

until twenty years after my decease'. Limited though these extracts are in terms of his lifetime they provide a clear enough picture of the man and his way of life, as well as his unusual spelling.

During 1765 Cole had been in Paris, returning in December to Dover, where he was laid up for a while due to an injury to his knee. He returned to Bletchley on New Year's Day 1766 as he recorded:

'Jan. 1. *Circumcision of our Lord*. Very fine day. I quitted St. Alban's, having had a good Night's Rest, about 11. & got . . . to the Parsonage at Blecheley about 3 o'Clock to Dinner: having bore my Journey as well as if nothing had happened. . . . The Ringers did me the honour to ring the Bells on my Arrival, & they all 8 came into the Kitchin, as usual with them 4 Times a Year, & drank as much as they pleased in Reason & Sobriety. . . . As I have for these 30 years kept a sort of Diary of the Weather & Journal of other Things, being as someone justly calls it, The Importance of a Man to his own Self, I shall 'till I am tired of it, transcribe from my Almanacks, the contents of them, & so run over the last year, & be ashamed of the Manner in which it has passed.'

As he settled in again various visitors called, including his lace-making neighbours, the Cartwright brothers, followed by Mrs Goodwin, the young wife of the neighbouring rector of Loughton, whose marital unrest was a byword in the district. He wrote:

'Saturday 18. Thaw. Mr. James Cartwright came from London & came to see me, ("as one of the brothers is always in Town, & the other in the Country to attend to their Lace-makers."). Mrs. Holt and Mrs. Goodwin drank Coffee with me; they both cried & told me of Mr. G's ill Humours at Home. . . . I gave them a Neat's Tongue which I had brought with me from Paris, & a Snuff Box for him, which I had in Purpose bought for him . . . on which were painted Turtle Doves Billing . . .'

He was a generous employer with a staff including a maid, several daily women, his 'man' Tom Wood, son of his parish clerk William Wood ('a quiet, good tempered Man, & no Fault but drunkenness.'), a gardener named Tansley, as well as other part-time workers, but his bachelor existence was not without domestic upsets, as for instance:

'Thursday 23. Thaw & Lowering. I found out to Day that my Maid, to whom I allowed handsome Board Wages in my Absence, the use of a Cow, Beer, Ale, Coals & Candles & other Things, with Half-a-Crown per Week, had not left me one Onyon or Potatoe, tho' there were 3 Bushells of the last and one of the former, when the Gardener brought them into the House for the Winter's use. I was very angry that none were left . . .'

His generosity made him a ready target for his needier friends, particularly Joe Holdom, his butcher. A typical entry in February read:

'Sunday 9. Thaw. After Matins I went to the other End of the Town to administer the Sacrament to Robert Ashby & to pray by Wm. Bradbury. I lent 6 Pounds to Joe Holdom the Butcher, & as many to Mr. Cartwright about a Fortnight ago . . .'[1]

In a March entry dated 'Monday 3.' he noted, without comment:

'Fine Day. I baptised Sarah, the Bastard Daughter of the Widow Smallwood of Eaton, aged near 50, whose husband died above a year ago.'

Despite a busy social life he was conscientious and fearless when his duty was involved as another March entry demonstrated:

'Thursday 20. Cold & dry. . . . I went in my Chaise to Eaton to pray by the wife of Robert King; from thence to West Blecheley on the same Errand to the Wife of Robert Mollard, very ill with a Cancer on her Thigh from thence to Robert Ashby, who is better, but I prayed by him, as I did also with Wm. Bradbury, who was very ill of Consumption.

I wrote to Mr. Etheridge of Simpson, Brother-in-Law to
Farmer Turner, who died at West Blecheley yesterday of the
Small Pox, to let him be put into the Grave this Evening, & I
would read the Burial Service over him to-morrow; as
hardly any of the Parish had had the Distmper & few of the
Clergy could be got to bury him; as even those who had had
it themselves, were afraid of carrying the Infection to their
Wives & Children. He readily assented to my Proposal;
Mrs. Willis[2] so alarmed, that she went out of the Parish for a
week or two.

'Friday 21. Dry & cold, but fine. . . . After Matins, I read
the Burial Service over the half-filled up Grave of Mr.
Turner. Mrs. Holt & her daughter Mrs. Goodwin, drank Tea
& Coffee with me. Mr. Tomkins of Newton grafted 2 Trees
in my Garden.'

In April he recorded yet another aspect of his parish work:
'Thursday 3. Rain & Snow. I made friends of Henry
Travel & Joseph Ray, our Turnpike Gate Keeper, who had
had a Quarrel. I wrote to Mr. White, Bookseller at *Horace's
Head* in Fleet Street, for near £4 worth of Books.'

He was not averse to criticising his superior clergy in
his diary and probably amongst his friends. In April he
wrote:

'. . . the clownish Carriage & Want of Behaviour &
Manners in the present Bp.[3] was so notorious at his last
Visitation that every one was scandalised at it, & among all
my Acquaintance I never heard him mentioned but with the
utmost Disrespect. . . . Indeed the Bp's ungainly, awkward,
splay-footed Carriage & Yorkshire Dialect is a full Indication
of his humble Education & mean Extraction . . .'

He continued with some vehemence:

'. . . With what Face can the Church of England abuse
the Popish Church & Hierarchy for Nepotism and Pluralities?
when they are equally if not greatly more guilty of the same
& other Faults, as pretending to a greater Purity, than the
other?'

In April he also revealed his political bias when he wrote:

'The Times are so hard, small Farms are so difficult to be met with, the Spirit of Inclosing, & accumulating Farms together, making it very difficult for young People to marry, as was used; as I know by Experience in this Parish, where several Farmer's Sons are forced to live at Home with their Fathers, tho' much wanting to marry & settle, for Want of proper Places to settle at. Which sufficiently shows the baneful Practice of Inclosures, & that the putting of the least Restraints upon Matrimony (as the last Marriage Act did, contrived by Lord Chancellor Hardwicke on selfish Family Motives as it was commonly said) is of great Disservice to the Nation.'

A further entry in April showed that an earlier strong reprimand to his parish clerk on drinking had had little effect:

'Sunday 20. Small Rain at Night, but fine Day. Will Wood so drunk that his Wife sent to me to desire that I would let Will Turpin officiate for him . . .'

Cole had a fondness for the entire Wood family and was prepared to forgive them a lot. Although abstemious himself he had a large man's tolerance for weakness in others, including drunkenness. This was summed up in a comment when his friend and neighbour Nathaniel Cartwright came home drunk from the Lace market at Newport Pagnell: 'Now & then he will get fuddled.'

In June came the rumbling prelude to an explosion which was to threaten Cole's peace of mind for some months:

'Friday 20. Fine Day. Some Rain. . . . Mr. Stevens of Fenny Stratford, who had 120 Sheep & 14 Horses in my Clay Pit Close a whole Night this Time Twelvemonth & did me 50s worth Damage (as by my Mowers' Account, it being just before mowing) yet would make me no Recompense, called on me to Day, as 16 of his Cows were in the same Close & did me 20s Damage, as by his own Confession. He came to thank me for bringing them into my yard & not pounding them, & desired to pay me for the Damage they had done me in my mowing Grass, I told him I would not settle with him for this, till he had made me Satisfaction for my last year's Suffering by him. He asked me what I demanded; I told him a Guniea; which he gave me; & I returned him half-a-Guinea back again . . .'

In August matters went from bad to worse:

'Saturday 9. Excessively hot. My little Horse being in Robert Stevens his Pasture, close to my Clay Pit Close, the Fence between us belonging to him . . . he carried it Home, sending me word, that I might have my Horse again if I would send the Half Guinea I took of him. . . . I sent Word to him by a short Letter, that I apprehended his Business was to see after his own Fences . . . therefore desired he would send me my Horse by my Servants or he should hear further from me. Accordingly it was sent . . .

'Sunday 10. Fine Day, but excessive hot. Mr. Stevens had my Coach Horse to F. Stratford Pound, where he was from before 6 in the Morning 'till 9 at Night . . . I never was more uneasy in my Life, having never had such an Insult & Affront offered to me & it was very unpleasant to me to. have any Squabbles with anyone, much more with my Parishioners.'

He decided . . . 'to throw up the Ground, tho' most convenient & serviceable to me, rather than be at eternal War with a litigious & spiteful Neighbour. . . . As I never yet had occasion to fee & consult a Lawyer, I was loth to do it against one of my Parishioners; & so am determined to sit down under my injury . . .'

Despite this decision, when Steven's horse was found in the disputed Clay Pit Close that night on Cole's ground, he ordered it to be put into his stables. The following morning he recorded:

'Tuesday 12. Gloomy cool Day. Mr. Stevens here before I was up, at 7 in the morning about his Horse. I endeavoured to convince him of the Malignity of his Disposition.

... The only excuse the Hog had to make was, that I had taken Half a Guinea of his Money, tho' he acknowledged even then, that it was not by half an Equivalent for the Damage . . . (for there was the Greivance with this greedy Fellow, who was your very humble Servant, if you would let him devour you & eat you up, but would do you all the Mischeif that laid in his Power if you resisted;) . . . I . . . told him even now, if he would ask my Pardon & say he was sorry for what he had done, I would excuse it, tho' I had his Horse in the Pound . . . which, with great Reluctance & Unwillingness he at last brought himself to do. . . . However I sent a letter to Mr. Cooke after Breakfast . . . to give him Notice of my Design to hold this most convenient Close no longer than Lady Day, as I could never be secure from the Insults & Ill Behaviour of so great a Brute. . . . But Hogs are the proper Comabatants with Hogs . . . I would not be concerned with such a Fellow upon any Terms . . .'

There was only one further entry on the subject in September:

'Thursday 4. Very fine Day. Stevens had 23 Sheep all Night in my Close, where they were found by John Holdom, who went early to get my horses, which I lent to his Father, with my cart. Stevens sent a Boy for his Sheep, but came not himslf . . .'

A few days later Cole was amply revenged:

'Tuesday 9. Very fine Day. . . . I went to Dinner at the *White Lion* at Little Brickhill, to meet the Justices who were to sign the Licences. . . . When Stevens of Fenny Stratford came in, I complained that he had done nothing to the Roads, & the Justices every one of them rebuked him for his ill Behaviour to me; I should not have mentioned it, had not Dr. Pettingal[4] asked if he was not the man that had pounded my Horses. . . . Jem[5] so drunk at the meeting, Mr. Knapp's servant carrying him to another Inn, that he followed us not Home; so that I sent Tom on one of the Coach Horses to look for him, who found him on the Road: and when he got

off his Horse, was not able to stand; so he well whipped him
& put him to bed.

'Wedn. 10. Wretched Day. Stormy & Rainy. Will Wood
came & whipped Jem handsomely. I told him to look out
for a Master for his Son, who would be spoiled with me . . .'

In the end Jem remained in Cole's service, along with the
indispensable Tom, and continued to be whipped regularly.
Meanwhile Cole continued on good terms with his neighbours the Cartwright brothers:

'Monday 15. Exceeding fine Day. . . . I dined at Mr. Cartwright's. . . . I got in my Hay very well. Ringing all Day. I
supped at Mr. Cartwright's.

'Wed. 17. . . . The greatest Filbert year every where that
was ever remembered; tho' there seems to be but few
Walnuts. . . . I carried a large Basket of Filberts to Mr. N.
Cartwright & drank Tea with him in his Garden; he spent
the Even with me, when I settled my Accounts with him &
paid him £11 17s 9d for Books & Things he had bought for
me in London.'

The giving and receiving of small presents was one of the
courtesies of the day and if due acknowledgement was not
made it could easily cause offence as in a case instanced by
Cole:

'Thursd. Oct 2. Very fine Weather. Mr. Taylor brought
me a fine Haunch of Venison: I sent directly to invite Mr.
Pitts[6] & his sister to Dinner & sent him 8 Pigeons as a
Present, they being remarkably & universally scarce this
year; when he came he had not the Civility to thank me for
them, or took the least Notice of them. I sent also to
Mr. & Mrs Sanderson, who sent me a very pretty Dish of
Tench . . .'

Towards the end of November came an entry concerning
his future at Blecheley. Cole had originally been presented
with the living in 1753 by the distinguished but eccentric
antiquarian Browne Willis, who had inserted a clause,
common in those days, reserving the living 'as a portion for

my grandson'. This did not affect Cole until the entail of the estate was cut by Browne Willis's grandson Thomas in order to leave the estate to his half-brother Jack, thus disinheriting his cousin Tom Willis who was otherwise next in line. In the circumstances Cole felt in duty bound in stand by his original bargain with Browne Willis, thus providing the disinherited and penniless grandson, Tom Willis, with a living, if he took Orders. Despite the arguments and persuasions of his friends and legal advisors, Cole quixotically stood by his word. He wrote:

'Sat. 29. . . . Dined at Mr. Pomfret's[7]: he advised me to have Mr. Cummin's Opinion. . . . I told him to please him I would, but that I was determined to resign at the Time. . . . I told him he might do as he pleased: especially if an Opinion that the Bond is not good would prevent Dilapidations & procure better Terms on the Resignation. I offered Mr. Promfret a 36s Peice, but he would not accept of it . . .'

The next day Cole sent Mr Pomfret a letter in which he wrote:

'. . . I must needs tell you, that however Mr. Cummins's Opinion may turn out, I am determined in my own how to act; which is to resign at the proper Time . . .'

He was soon engaged in trying to find somewhere to live when he was forced to leave the rectory and amongst others he approached his friends the Huddlestons, a noted Roman Catholic family, who lived at Sawston Hall near Cambridge. Mention of this was included in an entry dated January 1767:

'Wedn. 21. Thaw & some Rain. . . . Mr. Pomfret sent me an Hare; I return'd him a Goose. Letter from Mr. Ferdinand Huddleston that he had not been at Sawston for some Time . . . but that he had sent my Letter to his Priest, Father Champion, who would make all proper Enquiries & let me Know, & hoped I would make Sawston my Home when I went into Cambridgeshire . . .'

The last day of January had an entry concerning an

unusual treatment for his favourite 'little Horse':

'Sat. 31. . . . The Physic did not agree with my little Horse: forced to give him a Jolop in the Morn; & Gin after Dinner . . .'

By this time rumours about his future were rife in the county and early in February he recorded one such and his reactions:

'Thursd: 5. Cold & Foggy. Mrs Holt & Mrs Goodwin called on me before Dinner: Mrs Holt told me she heard that I was not to quit Blecheley, as Mr Tho: Willis would not go into Orders: I told her I knew nothing of it; but that I conceived that a Person over Head & Ears in Debt & [who] had nothing to live on but this Expectancy, would not be long in determining the Expediency & even Necessity of taking this Living I told her that if Mr. Goodwin would buy my Post Chaise I would let him have it for 40 Pounds. Mr. Sanderson called on me. I lent Joe Holdom 5 Guineas without taking a Receit as he promised to return it in a week or 10 Days. Fine Afternoon.'

Two days later came the sequel to his offer to Mr Goodwin:

'Sat: 7. . . . Mr. Goodwin called on me & he gave me £40 for my Chaise: I told him I would give him a Guinea back again; so that I lose only about £15 for the use of it for near 3 years . . .'

On the 1st of March he received a letter from his friend Mr Masters, rector of Landbeach and Waterbeach, concerning his property there:

'Saturday 1. St. David. Tolerable Day. Lr. from Mr. Masters of the Horrors of my Tenant Huckle's Situation, who says it is impracticable for him ever to go to my Farm at Frog Hall again, it [the floodwater] being 4 Feet in the House: he advises me to buy Wm. Symonds House & Farm together with Mrs Porter's Land . . .'

Meanwhile his garden at the rectory was apparently coming into flower as his entry a few days later made clear:

'Frid: 6. Fine Day and cold. . . . Mrs Willis & Mrs Barton came about Noon into my Yard to give a look at my Crocus's, Mezareons, & Hypateca's: I gave Mrs Willis some Pots of Auriculas & Precox Tulips . . .'

In April he was ill with a sore throat and recorded:

'Thursd: 23. St. George. Little Sleep from my sore Throat. Sent for Mr. Harness the Apothecary of Fenny Stratford, & was blooded & very faint after it, so went to Bed, where I was forced to continue till 6 at Night. My Arm bled again. Mr Barton,[8] who was at Mrs. Willis's in his way to Town, buried Mary Virgin, the Bastard Dau. of Su. Virgin. Mr. Cartwright spent the Ev: with me . . .'

Mrs Willis died in June and her son, who had taken the name of Fleming on inheriting a large estate in Lancashire, informed Cole that his cousin, Tom Willis, intended taking Orders immediately. Cole noted:

'Frid: 12. Cold Day, but warmer towards Noon, when Mr. Fleming called on me. . . . I then told him of my Design of resigning at the appointed Time; but . . . that as I was thoroughly satisfied the Bond was naught . . . I hoped . . . on any future Vacancy of this or any other of his Livings . . . he would think me a proper Subject for it . . .'

After burying Mrs Willis on the 13th of June, Cole went to Cambridge, to look over a house of Mr Huddlestone's at Duxford, but found he did not like it. By this time he was growing a little desperate as his diary showed. He wrote:

'Thursd: 18. Very fine day . . . left Sawston. . . . Found Mr. Masters . . . at Dinner tho' hardly one o'Clock. After Dinner we went to Waterbeche where he was new flooring the Parlour of the Vicarage House, which tho' small, inconvenient & wretched, yet I desired him to let me have as I could, on quitting Blecheley (till some other Place offered) live very well there; he much persuaded me to the contrary, thinking it too bad; but on my persisting to have it, he told me I might have the Care of the Church also, if I chose it, it not being far from the Church; that he gave 20 Guineas a

year & that he would let me have the House, a small close
by it & another at a little Distance from it for 6 Pounds a
year; so I concluded about it immediately, as I found it so
excessively difficult to suit myself with a small Purchase . . .'

From this point onwards decisions regarding his move
began to have an increasing effect on his life. He noted:

'Mond: 29. . . . [Tom Wood] . . . told me his Mother was
uneasy at the Thought of his leaving Blecheley. . . . I told
him I desired him to do as he pleased & to his own
advantage, tho' should be much concerned if he left me.
He is so Honest, sober & good. I shall never get one like
him . . .'

In early July Cole took the opportunity of speaking to Mr
Barton about looking after the Wood family after he had left
the district. He had a soft spot for all of them, particularly old
Mrs Page, Tom's grandmother, the matriarch of the family,
who was now near to death, and also, of course, the
drunken Will Wood, his clerk, for whom he had made
arrangements with Mr Fleming to be made gamekeeper
'with a gun'. He wrote:

'Frid: 10. Fine Day. Mrs. Page taken with a Palsy on her
left Side; I went & red Prayers by her. Will Wood senr. came
to thank me for speaking to Mr. Barton for him. I took an
opportunity to speak roundly to him of his Drunkenness,
which he promised to leave off; I don't believe a word of it; I
told him I did not think of keeping Jem, which he told Jem
of when he went into the Kitchin, who cried all Night, as
Tom told me the next Day.'

On Sunday he noted:

'Sund: 12. Very hot. At Matins & churched Daniel's
Wife. . . . Red Prayers to Mrs. Page & gave her Absolu-
tion . . .'

The old matriarch rallied, but relapsed again in August,
when Cole visited Waterbeach by arrangement and may
have begun to have early doubts about the wisdom of his
decision. He recorded:

'Wedn: 12. . . . got to Mr. Masters' at Landbeche at 8 or before. . . . Mr. Masters not well pleased that I came so late & did not come on Monday . . . & seemed to think Mrs Page's dying State . . . signified nothing.

'Thursd: 13. . . . The Town [Waterbeach], it seems, is above half full of Methodists . . . if I had known as much at first I believe I should not have thought of it.'

He went on, however, with the preparations for his move, including on the 10th of September writing to his successor at Oxford, asking if he wanted anything left and if in turn he would mind if Cole left 'some Grafts &c in the Garden . . . 'till another year'. It was not until the 24th of September that he noted receipt of a reply:

'. . . too civil & complimental, I am afraid, to be hearty & sincere, especially as he omits saying a Word about Dilapidations, the chief Thing I wrote to him about; he promises me the Living again if ever Fortune should raise him from above his present Condition . . . complains of the ill-natured Reports that have been spread thro' Bucks concerning him . . . offers to take any Furniture I shall leave.'

In October Mr Eyles, vicar of Bradwell, visited him and provided a sample of thoroughly scandalous clerical gossip as Cole noted:

'Sat: 17. . . . Mr. Eyles of Bradwell came to Dinner with me. . . . He told me a Deal of Scandal of other People, & forgot how the world talks of him; he said Goodwin lay with Mrs Holt & that Mrs G. told Frank that her husband lay in the same Bed with her for 3 Weeks together & never touched her; that Mr. Knapp & his wife lived very unhappily; that they neither spoke to one another or bedded together, sometimes for 3 weeks together; that the Widow Woods was a Kept Mistress & that Mr Pitts said that none of his neighbours except Dr. Pettingal was any Thing of a Scholar or that he could learn any Thing from; with Abundance of other Tittle Tattle. I told him of Mr Pitts's

former Behaviour to me[9] . . . & he seemed delighted with
the Acquisition . . .'

The round of lengthy farewells dragged on with a note
that his successor 'would demand no Dilapidations' that
bane of outgoing clerics. An entry for Thursday the 19th of
October read:

'Gloomy Day. . . . Mr & Mrs Lord of Mursley. Mr. Ja:
Cartwright & his Sister & with them Mr. Ashurst of London.
. . . They drunk me above a Dozen Bottles of Liquor, more
than any Company I ever entertained before.'

By Friday 6th of November all was ready:

'Mr. Ridgeway's Wagon & 2 Carts . . . set out early in the
Morning for Bedford, very heavily laden; 3 of my Boxes
weighing each about 800 weight apiece, being 3 of my
larger Book Cases. Two others I shall leave for my Successor in their Places; as also some Window Curtains &
other Things . . .'

The final day before departure was a whirlwind of
activities:

'Thursd: 19. Breakfasted with Mrs Holt & Mrs Goodwin
at Mr. Cartwright's. Mrs Holt gave me a shilling of K. Henry
II & 20d of King Charles I. Mr. Day the Auctioneer here all
Day apprising & numbering my Goods for Sale. Joe
Holdom paid me his £5 5s 0d & I paid him his Bill £13 8s
9d. I gave his Son John a Guinea & 6 Pewter Plates, odd
broken China & other Things; gave old Will Wood a Peice
of black Manchester cut Velvet for a waistcoat. Paid Will
Grace his Bill £0 17s 0d & gave him some old broken China
& other odd Things. Paid my Maid Sarah Turvey her wages
& gave her a Quarter of a Guinea & a Tea Pot & a Pair of
Scissors Mrs Joyne had left here. Wrote to Mr Barton, Mr
Rob Lowndes, Mr Pomfret, Dr. Forester. Drank Tea at Mr.
Cartwright's who promised to take an Acct of my Sale & to
receive the Money. Agreed with Mr Ridgeway to carry me a
Load of Goods in a Cart & 3 Horses to Waterbeche for £2
12s 6d . . . at the same Time my Waggon went. Packed up

all my Goods. Tansley & I got up most of the Shrubs & Flowers & trees which are to go to Waterbeche . . .'

The next day he left Blecheley for good 'at 9 o'Clock'. He spent the night at Biggleswade, arriving at Landbeche on Saturday 'my horses much tired'.

To anyone who knew them it must have been obvious that a row was inevitable between Cole and the masterful Mr Masters, although initially all appeared well enough. Cole wrote:

'Sund: 22. Fine Day. I officiated at Landbeche & Mr Masters at Waterbeche, where we both rode after Dinner to look at the Vicarage House, which I liked moderately well . . . but nothing was completed . . . every Thing left for me to finish & fit up, even the Partitions of the Chambers & Staircase &c . . .'

In early December he moved into the half-finished house and the rumblings preparatory to the inevitable explosion were soon obvious:

'Tuesd: 8. Very fine Day. Joyner making Blinds for the Windows. Carpenter making a Door out of the Stable into the Cow-Yard & finishing the Staircase. Masons plaistering the new Chamber. . . . I sent John Wilson to Mr Masters in the evening about a Casement to the new Chambers, for about 200 Bricks for the Sink & Gutter, and about the fences.; he sent a bouncing Message, that the Tenant was to do Fences, that he had no Casement, & that I might send my own Horses, if they were come back, or get others to fetch the Bricks, as his own Horses were employed. He also sent & took the Lock off the Gate of the Close & desired the Man to tell me to put one of my own on. These Things give me much uneasiness & a sad Presage of his rough & morose Manners.'

Thursday the 10th was deceptively peaceful. He recorded:

'Rainy at Times, but fine Day. Masons making a Gutter & Sink in the Brewhouse. . . . Married Wm. Baxter to Mary

Howell, 2 Methodists with whom this Parish swarms. . . .
Buried Mr. Jacklyn at 5 o'Clock.'

He was all set for the eruption and the next day it came:

'Frid: 11. Glorious fine Day thro' out. . . . Mr Masters
came by 9 o'Clock . . . I paid him . . . his Bill for Nails & 2
Locks. . . . I then told him I thought it best to know on what
Terms I was to be here, as I thought it very hard to find
Materials & pay Workmen & pay Rent for other People's
Houses & desired to know how much he expected; he told
me it was my own Fault, that he never advised my coming
here, but rather disuaded me from it, that what he had done
was out of Regard to me; that it would cost him £40, that his
Cart had been here 30 Times with Wood, Straw &c &
himself fatigued to Death. I found nothing was to be made
out of him, but that he had me in a cleft Stick, as he said he
could produce Letters in which I had desired him to do what
he was about. What nettled me most was, his ordering his
Servants to take away in his Cart 3 or 4 Peices of short
Wood & old, that would make Posts; I told him it was very
hard for him to use up near 100 of my new Elm, Ash & Oak
Boards about his House & not allow such poor Stuff to help
make out the Fences . . . I told Mr Masters of his brutish &
rough Carriage; he said he was not conscious of it; but
rather was determined not to have come here again so
soon, as I had told him last Time he was here, That there
was not to be two Masters in this House. Whatever I might
think, I am certain I never said so to him, or any one else. I
told him he was mistaken if he thought I came here in any
other Light than his Equal, & that I would not be bullyed or
hectored at by him, & would not be his underling. He gave
my Servant Tom half-a-Crown.'

It had not taken Cole long to tame his landlord, for after
this onslaught they lived amicably enough as neighbours.
Nor was he long in settling into much the same routine as
before. Tom and his brother Jem, still with him, looked after
his house and horses. With the Cambridge Colleges close at

hand he was now able to enjoy the pleasures of the Common Room and evenings of learned discourse spiced with academic gossip. Despite his Methodist neighbours, who were also soon tamed, it is easy to visualise the benevolent, portly antiquary exchanging letters with his old schoolfellow Walpole and enjoying his urbane, peaceful, existence.

## NOTES

1 See Saturday 18th January.
2 Widow of Squire.
3 John Green, Bishop of Lincoln, son of a tax-collector from Yorkshire.
4 Prebendary of Lincoln, fellow antiquarian and Welshman, whom Cole cordially detested.
5 Tom Wood's younger brother also in Cole's service.
6 Rector of Great Brickhill.
7 His elderly solicitor friend in Newport Pagnell.
8 Son-in-law of Mrs Willis, in Holy Orders.
9 See p. 96.

# 7

## The Rev. James Woodforde

*Dinner to day boiled Beef & Goose rosted &c.*

James Woodforde (1740-1803) was born at Ansford in Somerset, where his father was rector. He was educated at Winchester and went on to Oxford. His diary starts on July 1st 1759, when he was just nineteen, with the brief entry: 'Made a scholar at New College.' For the next forty-three years he wrote almost daily accounts of his activities, filling, in the process, twenty-one volumes.

In 1763 he was ordained and returned to the West Country to act as his father's curate until the latter's death in 1771. There followed a period of uncertainty, while he continued as curate, during which time he met a Miss Betsy White in Shepton Mallett and wrote of her:

'September 25. . . . She is a sweet tempered girl indeed, and I like her very much, and I think would make a good wife. I do not know but I shall make a bold stroke that way . . .'

Throughout 1772 he remained at Ansford as curate, but in July 1773 the living was granted to a cousin and James Woodforde decided to leave the neighbourhood and take a post as sub-warden at New College. He still remained

*The late fifteenth-century beautifully preserved rood screen much as it was when the Rev. James Woodforde preached at Weston Longville in the latter part of the eighteenth century.*

enamoured of Miss White, however, and noted:

'Aug. 24. . . . I called at Mrs White's and stayed with her and her daughter Betsy till 8 o'clock. . . . Betsy White came from London only last Saturday. She is greatly improved and handsomer than ever . . .'

Nevertheless he soon settled comfortably into the bachelor routine at Oxford. On Christmas Day he described the College banquet with that loving exactitude which was to characterise all his entries on food:

'Dec. 25. . . . We had for dinner, two fine Codds boiled with Fryed Souls round them and oyster sauce, a fine sirloin of beef roasted, some peas soup and an orange Pudding for the first course, for the second, we had a leash of Wild Ducks rosted, a fore Qu: of Lamb and sallad and mince Pies. We had a grace cup before the second course. . . . After the second course there was a fine plumb cake. . . . After Grace is said there is another Grace-cup to drink. . . . We dined at 3 o'clock and were an Hour and a ½ at it.'

In November of the following year, 1774, he recorded:

'Nov. 5. . . . The Warden received an account of the Death of Mr Ridley, Rector of one of our Livings in Norfolk, by name Weston Longeville worth it is said £300 per annum . . .'

In December he wrote:

Dec. 6. . . . Master Senr. publickly declared this after-noon in the S.C.R. his intention of not taking the living at Weston. I therefore immediately being the next Senior in Orders canvassed the Senior Common Room and then went with the Master into the Junr Common Room and canvassed that. The Junr Common Room pretty full . . .'

His rival for the living was named Hooke, but Woodforde noted:

'Dec. 15. . . . We had a meeting of the whole House in the Hall at 12 o'clock, to present a Person to the Living of Weston Longeville. . . . Hooke and myself were the two candidates proposed . . . after 2 hours debate the House divided and it was put to the Vote, when there appeared for me 21 votes, for Mr Hooke 15 only. . . . I treated the Senr Common Room with Wine and Fruit in the afternoon and in the evening with Arrac Punch and Wine . . . after 11 o'clock I went down into the Junr Common Room . . . till after 12 and returned then to the Senr Common Room and stayed till near 4 o'clock. We were exceeding merry . . .'

In April of the following year 1775 he set off with an Oxford friend, Cooke, to visit Weston Longville. He recorded:

'April 10. I breakfasted in my room this morning at 7 o'clock upon some chocolate as did Cooke with me. After breakfast about 8 o'clock I set off in Jones's Post Coach for the City of London. Cooke went with me in the same and I promised to frank him all the way to Norfolk as he goes to oblige me . . .'

He started by attending the Bishop of Norwich in Upper Grosvenor Street to receive his Letters of Institution. Even though they were forced to wait two days before seeing the bishop it is clear that Woodforde was viewing the world through rose-tinted spectacles. He wrote:

'April 12. . . . I went to the Bishop of Norwich this morning, found his Lordship at home. Dr Salter with him, recd my Letters of Institution and was instituted very soon, his Lordship behaved exceeding handsome and free. Paid his Secretary, Mr Burn, for the same 4.17.6. Gave his Lordship's servant 0.5.0. The Bishop . . . is a short fat man . . .'

On April 13th in a 'hired Post Chaise and four' they set off for Norwich, leaving early in the morning and arriving after ten. He wrote feelingly:

'It being after 10 when we got to Norwich we found the City Gates shut. We did not get to bed till after 2 in the morning.'

Even so the mood of euphoria persisted and he wrote:

'April 14. We breakfasted, dined, supped and slept at Norwich. We took a walk over the City in the morning and we both agreed that it was the finest City in England by far . . .

'April 15. . . . about 12 we set out for my Living at Weston in a Chaise. . . . We got to Weston which is about 9 miles from Norwich by 2 o'clock in the afternoon, where we dined, supped and slept at the Parsonage House. To Turnpike and Driver from Norwich to Weston pd 2.0. My Curate Mr Howes came to us in the afternoon. Bed etc., all in readiness for us when we came. We carried with us some Wine and Cyder from Norwich.

'April 16. We breakfasted, supped and slept at Weston Parsonage. . . . We went to Church this morning at Weston and Cooke read Prayers and preached for Mr Howes. I also administered the H: Sacrament this morning at Weston Church being Easter Day — I had near 40 Communicants. . . . My clerk is a shocking Hand. The worst singing I ever heard in a Church, only the Clerk and one man, and both intolerably bad. . . . Cooke likes my House and Living very much. For my part I think it is a very good one indeed . . .'

During the next few days they explored the surroundings and Woodforde was inducted by Mr Howes. An estimate of the dilapidations was set at the high figure of £175 2s. 6d. Finally in May Woodforde returned to Oxford with his friend. In July he set off to the West Country on a visit to Ansford, no doubt congratulating himself on the fact that at last he had something to offer the woman he had in mind to marry. Two entries in August and in September speak for themselves:

'August 10. . . . Jenny Clarke returned from Devonshire last night. Betsy White of Shepton is to be married in a fortnight to a Gentleman . . . by name Webster . . . reported to have 500 Pd per annum, 10,000 Pd in Stocks. . . . He has settled 300 Pd per annum on Betsy.

'Sep. 16. . . . Mr & Mrs Webster (late Betsy White) came to Sister White's on Horseback this morning, and they dined and spent the afternoon there. . . . I did not go to Mrs

White's today, tho' much pressed in the aft: . . . took a walk in the evening . . . we met Mr & Mrs Webster in the Turnpike Road. Mrs Webster spoke as usual to me, but I said little to her, being shy, as she has proved herself to me a mere Jilt . . .'

This one near-venture into matrimony seems to have confirmed him in his bachelor ways. Returning to the University in October he was soon immersed in his duties there. A letter in November brought unwelcome news from Weston Longville on the subject of the dilapidations:

'Nov. 18. . . . Had a letter this evening from my Norfolk Curate who acquainted me that Mrs Ridley had had a survey taken on her side concerning Delapidations by a Clergyman, the Revd. Mr Du Quesne and a William Tompson, Carpenter at Hockering and they did not bring it to more than £26.9.0. N.B. a very wide difference between us indeed. My Curate Mr Howes is very much for Mrs Ridley.'

After a final round of banquets at Oxford, lovingly recounted, Woodforde returned to Somerset to wind up his affairs at Ansford. From February to May he was extremely busy. At last on 6th May he sent off seven large boxes of belongings to Norfolk. His final entry there read:

'May 9. . . . This morning at 9 O'clock took my final leave of the old Parsonage House at Ansford . . . about 10 o'clock I took my leave of my Friends at Ansford and set forth on my mare for Norfolk, and Bill Woodforde[1] and my boy Will. Coleman went with me. I left my friends very low on the occasion.'

They stopped at Oxford to wind up his affairs there and at last on May 20th he noted:

'. . . about 10 took my final leave of my Rooms at College and we set forth for Norfolk, myself, Bill Woodforde and my serv: Will Coleman . . .'

On the 24th of May they arrived at Weston Longville, where they found nothing to eat, so they rode to Lenwade

Bridge a mile further on and dined there. 'My servant Will supped and slept there. Myself and Bill supped and slept at Weston at my House.'

For the next few days he and his nephew were extremely busy buying essential household supplies in Norwich, setting a reliable ratcatcher to work and hiring maidservants. He wrote:

'June 3. . . . Two servant maids came to me this morning and offered their services to me. I agreed with them both and they are to come to me here Midsummer day next. One of them is to be an upper servant and she lived very lately with Mrs Howes. A very pretty woman she is and understands cooking and working at her needle well. I am to give her per annum and tea twice a day — 5.5.0. She was well recommended to me by Mrs Howes and the reason she was turned away from Mrs Howes was her not getting up early enough . . .'

In the midst of all this he was laid low with toothache:

'June 4. I breakfasted, dined, supped and slept again at Weston. My tooth pained me all night, got up a little after 5 this morning & sent for one Reeves a man who draws teeth in this parish, and about 7 he came and drew my tooth, but shockingly bad indeed, he broke away a great piece of my gum and broke one of the fangs of the tooth it gave me exquisite pain all the day after, and my Face was swelled prodigiously in the evening and much pain. Very bad and in much pain the whole day long. Gave the old man that drew it however 0.2.6. He is too old, I think, to draw teeth, can't see very well.'

As if this were not enough there followed one of those domestic upsets which anyone who has kept dogs will recognise:

'June 5. . . . Very much disturbed in the night by our dog which was kept within doors tonight, was obliged to get out of bed twice or thrice to make him quiet, had him into my room, and there he emptied himself all over the room. Was obliged to order him to be turned out which Bill did. My face much swelled, but rather easier than yesterday tho' now very tender and painful, kept in today mostly. Paid and gave Will my servant this evening 0.5.0. Paid Mr Dunnell this evening part of a bill due to him from me, for 2 cows, 3 Piggs, 3 pr. Shoes, Flower, Tea, Sugar, News Papers, Pipes, Candles, Pan, Tobacco, Beer, Mustard, Salt, Washing, Halters, Comb and Brush, Crabs, Bread and Porterage of £14.9.3. the sum of a Bank Note — of £10 0 0.'

It was not long before he found himself involved in local affairs and gossip:

'July 19th. . . . Bill and myself took a ride in the afternoon to Mr Howes at Hockering where we spent the remaining part of the afternoon with Mr Howes and his Wife. Mr Howes went to bury a corpse for Mr du Quesne and when he was gone Mrs Howes told us she lived very unhappy with her Husband as he wants her to make her Will and give everything to his family. I advised her to the contrary, and to give to her own. We were wet coming back as it rained.'

The subject of dilapidations still caused trouble. He noted:

'Sept. 4th. . . . Mr Francis Junr. of Norwich my Attorney came to my House this morning to shew me a letter . . . from Mrs Ridley in which she mentions that she cannot comply with the last Estimate . . . therefore I advised Mr Francis to apply to my Proctor . . . to begin the suit . . . Mr Custance the Squire's brother sent me a brace and a half of Partridges this evening. Very kind of him.'

Later that month his harvest was finally got in and he wrote:

'Sept. 14th. . . . Very busy all day with my Barley, did not dine till near 5 in the afternoon, my Harvest Men dined here to-day, gave them some Beef and some plumb Pudding and as much liquor as they would drink. This evening finished my Harvest and all carried into the Barn —

8 acres. I had Mrs Dunnell's Cart and Horses and 2 men yesterday and to-day. The men were her son Thomas and Robin Buck . . .'

He arranged a good feast for the people paying his tithes:

'Dec. 3rd. . . . My Frolic for my People to pay Tithe to me was this day. I gave them a good dinner, surloin of Beef rosted, a Leg of Mutton boiled and Plumb Puddings in plenty. Recd. to-day only for Tithe and Glebe of them . . . 236.2.0 Mr Browne called on me this morning and he and myself agreed and he paid me for Tithe only 55.0.0 included in the above, he could not stay to dinner. They all broke up about 10 at night. Dinner at 2. Every Person well pleased, and were very happy indeed. They had to drink Wine, Punch, and Ale as much as they pleased; they drank of wine 5 Bottles, of Rum 1 gallon and half, and I know not what ale. Old Harry Andrews, my clerk, Harry Dunnell and Harry Andrews at the Heart all dined, etc. in Kitchen. Some dined in the Parlour and some in the Kitchen 17 dined etc. that paid my Tithe. . . . Mr Peacement came just at dinner time, but he had dined; he spent the afternoon and evening however. There was no supper at all provided for them. We had many droll songs from some of them. I made use of about 13 lemons and about 2 Pds of sugar. Bill and myself both well tired when we went to bed.'

December was a crowded month. On the 11th he recorded satisfaction finally reached for both sides on the vexed subject of the dilapidations. On the 13th he noted:

'Dec. 13th. . . . This day being appointed a Fast on our Majesty's arms against the rebel Americans I went to Church this morning and read the Prayers appointed for the same. I had as full a congregation present as I have in the afternoon on a Sunday, very few that did not come . . .'

Just before Christmas he wrote with satisfaction:

'Dec. 23rd. . . . I had a very fine Turkey for dinner to-day, and the best I ever tasted in my life . . .'

By this time it would appear that the local tradesmen and

others had begun to suspect that the quickest way to their rector's heart was through his stomach. He recorded:

'Dec. 25th. . . . Mr. Brooke my Upholsterer sent over a Man on purpose from Norwich this morning with a fine Hind Quarter of London Lamb, prodigious fine it was indeed. I gave the man some victuals and drink and 0.1.0. The undermentioned poor old People dined at my House to-day being Christmas Day and went to Church with me in the afternoon, to each of them gave 0.1.0. [There follows a list of seven names, including James Smith the clerk.] By God's blessing I intend doing the same next Christmas Day. Gave old Richard Bates an old black coat and waistcoat. I had a fine sirloin of Beef rosted and Plumb Puddings. It was very dark at Church this aft. I could scarce see . . .'

In January he joined a local dining club, as he explained:

'Jan. 13th. . . . Went on my Mare and my servant Will: with me to Mr. Du Quesne's where I dined and spent the afternoon and stayed till 8 at night with him, Mr. and Mrs Howes and Mr. Donne. We had for dinner a Leg of Mutton boiled, a butter Pudding, and a couple of Ducks. It is a Clubb meeting and goes by the name of Rotation. I became a Member of it to-day and they all dine with me on Monday next. Every Monday is the day. At Quadrille this afternoon — lost 0.1.3. I gave nothing at all to the Servants.

'As there was no Moon to come home by, it was very dis-agreeable to come home thro' the Wood that I did, but I thank God I got safe and well back tho' very dark. When there is no Moon for the future will get back before it is dark.'

He recorded his first club meeting in his house as follows:

'Jan. 20th. . . . Mr. du Quesne, Mr Howes and Mr Donne dined and spent the afternoon with us being my Clubb day. I gave them for dinner a couple of Rabbits smothered with onions, a Neck of Mutton boiled and a Goose rosted with a Currant Pudding and a plain one. They drank Tea in the afternoon, played a pool of Quadrille after, drank a glass or two of Punch and went away about 8 o'clock. No Supper is a Rule. And no vails to servants, however Mr Donne gave 0.1.0 to my servant Will. The other two gave nothing. . . . At Quadrille this evening lost . . . 0.0.3.'

Amongst his daily entries in March was one concerning the case of the notorious Rev. Dr William Dodd (1729-1777) who was a highly popular preacher in London and also tutor to Philip Stanhope, Lord Chesterfield's godson. In February he had forged a bond in Lord Chesterfield's name, was tried, found guilty and in June was hanged, despite a public outcry led by Dr Samuel Johnson. It would seem Dr Woodforde was not amongst his supporters for he merely noted:

'March 1. . . . Dr. Dodd for forging a Bond on Ld. Chesterfield for 4000 Pd was tried this week and by the Jury brought in guilty. He is a Dr. of Divinity and late Chaplain to his Majesty.'

With occasional entries on current affairs, with infrequent journeys to Oxford or even down to Somerset, his diary continued its catalogue of parish work, farming, gardening and the social round, interspersed with births, deaths, marriages and visits to Norwich and always recurring details of the ample meals he ate. It was not very long before he parted from his nephew Bill, who was replaced by his niece, Nancy Woodforde. She remained with him as his housekeeper for the rest of his life and they settled down together very happily. In this way his routine was established with the annual tithe dinners providing a regular feature to mark the passage of time, when Nancy generally 'dined in the Study . . . by herself'.

There were, of course, numerous entries of general interest in the daily routine and Woodforde's benevolent attitude to his parishioners and others was particularly noticeable. For instance, in 1787 when his niece Nancy had been ill for some time, but was beginning to recover, he wrote:

'Jan. 25. . . . Nancy had a very indifferent Night and rather worse to-day, being still weaker. She did not come down Stairs till 2 o'clock this afternoon. However she made a good Dinner on a boiled Leg of Mutton and Caper Sauce and was better after. Rode to Ringland this Morning and married one Robert Astick and Elizabeth Howlett by Licence, Mr. Carter being from home and the Man being in Custody, the Woman being with Child by him. The Man was a long time before he could be prevailed on to marry her when in the Church Yard; and at the Altar behaved very unbecoming. It is a cruel thing that any Person should be compelled by Law to marry. I received of the Officers for marrying them 0.10.6. It is very disagreeable to me to marry such Persons. . . . At Cribbage this Evening with Nancy won 0.2.0. So that she owes me now at Cards 0.13.0. Nancy was a good deal better this Evening.'

In 1788 George III fell seriously ill. In March 1789 Woodforde noted:

'March 8. Sunday. . . . I read Prayers and Preached this afternoon at Weston Church — Also read with the greatest Pleasure a Prayer composed on the Occasion of the Restoration of his Majesty's Health, which I received this Morning. I return also to thee O Lord my private but most unfeigned Prayer of Thanksgiving for the same. And may so good a King long live to reign over us . . .'

It is surprising at first sight how much more bucolic Woodforde's life was, compared for instance with that of Cole, who was only something like a further hundred miles south-west. It is noticeable, however, that compared with the more scholarly Ridpath, or the more sophisticated Cole, Woodforde did not read a great deal beyond the daily newspapers and occasional novels, such as *Tom Jones*. If not socially engaged he passed the evenings playing games such as cribbage with his niece, Nancy. Out of doors, during the day, he was engaged in farming, or gardening, or occasionally coursing. Apart from that, of course, his constant interest was food and drink, although his strongest comment on the latter was: 'Very heavy all day, by sitting up so late and drinking more than usual last Night, tho' not the least disguised by it.' Yet not even his tithe banquets can account for all the brandy, rum, gin and wine he chronicled receiving.

In common with all his neighbours, including no doubt Squire Custance, Woodforde patronised his local smuggler as a matter of course for such taxed items as rum, gin, tobacco, silk and tea. Thus in 1792 he was extremely worried when he feared the excise men were on his trail, as he recorded:

'Sep. 15. Saturday. . . . Had a Tub of Rum brought me this Evening.

'Sept. 16. Sunday. . . . We were much agitaged this Evening about what I had brought me Yesterday. Bad reports about the Parish.

'Sep. 17. Monday. . . . I got up very early this Morning and was very busy all the Morn' in a very necessary business. . . . Dinner to-day boiled Beef very salt indeed, very much out of sorts — much jaded and had [no] Appetite. Mem. Jno Norton is supposed to have informed against his neighbour Buck.'

Buck was the principal local smuggler and no doubt the 'nesessary business' was burying the illicit rum and removing all traces of any other smuggled goods on the premises. In the circumstances it was very understandable that he felt 'out of sorts' since he was no doubt wondering how far Norton's indiscretions had extended. Within three weeks, however, he had recovered sufficiently to enjoy a day's coursing.

'Octob. 9. Tuesday. . . . Soon after breakfast I walked out a coursing with my People, and with 3 Greyhounds and 3 Spaniels, ran three Hares and killed two of them — the Hare that got off shewed the best Sport, being started on Ringland Brakes. Those that we killed shewed good Sport. We returned home before 3 o'clock. Gave to a Boy keeping sheep on Ringland Brakes, that informed us there was a Hare lately seen by him on the same, and which was started and gave her a good sweating, tho's she got away, as she deserved, gave him 0.6. N.B. The first Day of my going out a coursing this Season, very great Sport.'

Three days later he noted that his local smuggler was fined in court without further revelations:

'Oct. 12. Friday. . . . John Buck, the blacksmith, who was lately informed against for having a Tub of Gin found in his House that was smuggled, by Two Excise Officers, was pretty easy fined. Dinner to day boiled Tongue and Turnips and a fine Couple of Ducks rosted.'

Doubtless Squire Custance was on the bench imposing the fine on his principal supplier and it was probably not long before John Buck's customers, including Parson Woodforde, had seen to it that he was not seriously out of pocket and started buying fresh supplies, for instance:

'Oct. 20. Saturday. . . . To my Blacksmith Jno Buck, my annual Bill for divers little matters done for me pd him 1.13.3.

'Oct. 22. Monday. . . . Had a Tub of Gin this Evening.

'Oct. 23. Tuesday. . . . Did not get up till 9 o'clock this morning, then bottled off my Gin recd last Night, and soon after breakfast dressed and set off in my little Curricle for Norwich at 11 o'clock, got there before one — went to Mr. Priest's Senr. paid him a Bill for Wine to the sum of 13.0.6. Then went to Miss Brownes and paid a Bill for Nancy, for which she gave me Cash 2.15.6. For Oysters and Porter at Norwich, pd. 0.3. To 100 Walnuts pd 1.0. To Bury Pears at 3 a penney pd. 1.0. To 3 Dozen of Waistcoat Buttons, pd. 1.6. To 5 lb ½ of Glocester Cheese at 6d pd 2.9. To Frank, my Barber at the Kings-Head for his Master D. Callington for a new Wigg has some little time back pd 1.1.0. Gave Frank for himself 1.0. Saw Mr Du Quesne at Mr. Priests. . . . For Herrings at Beal's 18 — pd 0.6. Got safe and well home (thank God) dinner on Pork Stakes. A most delightful Day we had indeed. Nancy having a Cold could not go with me. Briton only went with me in the Curricle. . . . To Will: Large's Wife who brought me a Leveret, gave 1.0d. Had a Tub of Brandy and a Tub of Rum brought this Evening. Gave one of the Men that brought it 1.0.

'Oct. 24. Wednesday. . . . Very busy between 8 and 10 o'clock this Morn in bottling off Brandy and Rum . . .

He maintained close contact with his relations in Somer-set as he duly chronicled, as for instance, in 1794:

'Aug. 9. Saturday. . . . Betty Cary brought our Newspapers &c., from Norwich. Nancy had by her a Letter from Jenny Pinsett, in which was a ten Pound Bank of England Bill, for me from Mr. Pounsett,[2] in part of Rent due to me from Somersett Tenants at Ansford & c. £10.0.0. All our Friends tolerably well in Somersett.'

So the years passed with his social round, his parish duties, the dinners and similar breaks in the routine, all meticulously noted. In 1797, however, he was seriously ill for some time and his life was in danger. His diary was continued on separate sheets of paper but despite everything he started to recover once again. It is striking that even in his worst periods the details of his meals are always entered carefully. Typical entries at this period were:

'June 22. Thursday. . . . Dinner to day a rosting Pig &c. I think I am gaining strength, but still weak — App. good.

'Aug. 21. Monday. . . . Very poorly again this Morning rather weaker. Dinner to day. Leg of Mutton rosted &c. Rather ticklish weather for the Harvest . . .

'October 19. Thursday. . . . Had a very good Night and found myself stronger rather this Morning but excessive weak on stooping. . . . Dinner to day boiled Beef & Goose rosted &c. Appetite I think a little better for the last 2 Days.'

From this point onwards he scarcely looked back and for the next four years continued his life in the same old pattern. In July 1802, however, he had a violent throat infection and although he partially recovered and continued entries in his diary the end was not far off. His final entry ended on a familiar note:

'October 17. Sunday. We breakfasted, dined. Very weak this Morning, scarce able to put on my Cloaths and with great difficulty, got down Stairs with help. Mr Dade read Prayers & Preached this Morning at Weston Church — Nancy at Church. Mr. & Mrs Custance & Lady Bacon at Church. Dinner to day, Rost Beef &c.'

On Saturday, January 1st 1803 James Woodforde died in his sixty-third year, deeply mourned by his loving niece, Nancy, and no doubt also by many of his parishioners and friends in the parish of Weston Longville.

## NOTES

1 His nephew, who was to act as his companion.
2 His brother-in-law.

# 8

## The Rev. William Jones

### Henpecked Curate and Vicar: Hertfordshire

*I am now in the nineteenth year of my servitude*

The Rev. William Jones (1755-1821) had a humble Methodist upbringing in Abergavenny, but was well-educated at the local Grammar school and won a scholarship to Jesus College, Oxford. After a period in Jamaica as tutor to the sons of Thomas Harrison, the Attorney General, he returned to England in 1780, completed his degree and was ordained. In 1781 he accepted the post of curate of Broxbourne in Hertfordshire. He first started keeping a diary in Jamaica and continued to do so with occasional lapses for the rest of his life. The resultant 2,962 pages were edited in 1928 by his great-grandson, O.F. Christie.

On 3rd May 1781 Jones wrote:

'How happy, I had almost said blest, shall I be, says my heart, when in possession of a dear partner! . . . I have my eye upon a Lady of Waltham Abbey . . .'

His marriage is not recorded for there are twenty-five pages missing from his diary at this point, but he became curate of Broxbourne on 3rd June 1781 and soon afterwards married Theodosia Jessop, daughter of a solicitor in Waltham Abbey. Early in the New Year of 1782 he recorded:

'Jan. 3rd 1782. I have entered on a new year. . . . That I

*The church at Broxbourne and the vicarage alongside it remain surprisingly unchanged from the late eighteenth century and would easily be recognised by the Rev. William Jones, even if Broxbourne itself has changed beyond all recognition.*

am married, happily married, to one who is so good a woman, must in chief, take the lead of all other temporal mercies in my hands. May I never undervalue this blessing! I am employed as a Clergyman, & in every respect comfortably situated. May God, if it be His Will, continue to me and my dearest Theodosia in our present mercies!'

In June of 1782 their first child was born, to be followed in 1783 by another. In April 1784 he wrote ruefully:

'Sunday Apl. 11th. Easter. Providence seems now to frown on me & to blast all my schemes — An increasing family & a decreasing income. What is to be done? Where is Ign$^s$ Sancho's maxim "The more children, the more blessings"? I will not despair. It struck a damp on my spirits yesterday, when, on casting up my accts. I found that the expences of the last quarter exceed 36£ which sum is double my income for the same quarter.'

As may be imagined he was extremely busy trying to make ends meet by taking pupils and teaching to augment his curate's income during the next few years and his diary was consequently neglected. He noted:

'1786. Sept. 3rd. What a vast chasm from June 1785 to Sep. 1786. I really believe that my neglecting to journalise has very much contributed to my soul's decline in spiritual things!'

Nevertheless there was another gap until November 1787:

'Friday Nov. 28th. Since I wrote last my mind has been much disturbed by a difference which took place between Mrs J — & myself: &, what is still worse, we carried it to very high words in the presence of Miss R.A. Muller and both assistants. The origin of it was my insisting on dining at 1 o'clock, which I find the most convenient time for my school.

'I wish I could never lose sight of what Lord Chesterfield has strongly recommended     "Fortiter in re, suaviter in modo . . ."

'I can truly say . . . I wish everyone about me to be happy; but my temper is alas! too warm & hasty. And my *Dosy's* temper is too much like mine in this respect. Every misunderstanding we have I sincerely wish may be our last. But I too soon forget my good . . . resolutions . . .'

By 1791 he admitted to being a very henpecked husband. He wrote:

'Sunday 20th Feby. 1791. . . . My wife & I (for let me not forget to give precedency to whom precedency is due), seem to be disputing about the mastery. At the end of every contention, I am ready to say — "Let me submit, since you will not."'

On the death of the incumbent, George Stockwell Jr., in 1794, Jones was not fortunate enough to obtain the living, which went instead to the Rev. John Nesbit Jordan. Although Jones tried to obtain other livings he was unsuccessful. His family had meanwhile increased to ten and his school's fortunes waxed and waned. He remained henpecked. In 1799 he recorded:

'Saty. June 29th. . . . Clerical Chronology can, I think, hardly record more instances like that of the poor Curate of Broxbourn. This is my first curacy — I am now in the nineteenth year of my servitude; for I believe it is usually called *serving* a cure, or curacy, & to the very best of my recollection, or my clerk's, two, or at most three, Sundays are all that I have ever been absent from my parish in that time. And I ought to add, with humble yet cheerful gratitude, that I have been indulged by Heaven with a more than common share of good health.'

By 1800 he was seriously contemplating throwing up his curacy, but in March he gave up the idea at his wife's urging, noting:

'Mar. 30th. . . . My *dear* wife is a lawyer's daughter, & possesses such a wonderful volubility of speech, such a miraculous power of twirling & twisting every argument to her own interests, that I am no match for her *High Mighti-*

*ness.* She right well knows how "to puzzle right, & varnish wrong." No Old-Bailey solicitor, no *puzzle-cause* throughout the Kingdom, better knows this sublime art.

'Whether she has by dint of application, or in the management of me, acquired this facility, I know not . . .'

At this period one of Jones's greatest burdens was the principal parish officer, a man named Rogers, Lord Monson's steward. When the Rev. J.N. Jordan announced his intention of retiring in 1801 Rogers did all in his power to prevent Jones gaining the living. Jones wrote of him:

'April 29th 1801. . . . If there is a greater *rogue & villain* than ordinary, he obtains the honourable post of tax-gatherer, etc. & usually elbows & shoulders himself into the chief parish-offices. . . . As Overseer, he may enter into his acct. many shillings, as if given for occasional relief of the poor, which shillings never escaped from his clutches. To others, he pretends to give part of their allowance in poor, watery, half rotten potatoes . . . for which he will take care to charge an uncommonly high price. The above is a likeness taken from real life — I hardly need add whose likeness it is.'

When a day later Rogers raised a petition to the bishop opposing Jones's nomination for the living and allowed his cattle to trample Jones's fields their feud boiled over. On May 1st Jones wrote furiously:

'Fiend Rogers, [sic]

Your horses & other cattle are in my fields every night. I know they must be *turned in.* It is of no use to mend the hedges, for tho' done thoroughly, on Saturday last, by a man who shall appear as a witness, the stakes & thorns were pulled up, *designedly* by one o'clock on Sunday. I chased the horses out, on Wednesday night, with a view to pound them; tho' when your boy was told by the carter they were in the fields, he pretended not to believe him. I have put in nothing since Xmas & your cattle have entirely spoilt the crop. You will soon hear from Mr Jessop on the subject, &

in spite of your pretended consequence I will convince you
that you have no more right to let your beasts stray about the
roads & commit trespass in consequence, than the poorest
wretch in the parish. I am now actually preparing instruc-
tions for my Attorney & Counsel for a cause of still greater
importance to you, wherein, I trust, you will be made to
smart with exemplary damages.'

Poor Jones must have been near to a nervous breakdown
at this stage as extracts from a letter the same day to Mr
Jordan seem to show:

'My dear Sir,

When I parted from you last you were so good as to say
you hoped I should soon have an agreeable summons to
Town. I am quite unable to describe to you what I feel in my
present state of suspense. . . . As soon as his Lordship
declared his benevolent intentions towards me . . . I had no
doubt on the subject. . . . But how shall I tell you? If the
bragging of my good friend, Mr Rogers, be true, he has
according to his own phrase, *done my business with the
Bishop* — by writing a letter full of calumnies & misrepre-
sentations, & by inducing a person to second his efforts. . . .
The man who keeps the alehouse opposite Mr Rogers's, &
where he spends a great part of his time, called on me . . .
that Rogers had left a copy of his letter to the Bishop on the
table in the public house. The landlord of the Bull soon
afterwards assured me Mr. R. had communicated the same
to him, for such people are his chief confidants . . .'

Fifteen years later, on glancing through his diary, Jones
was suprised to notice how much he had written about
'John Rogers, the most *outrageous* of all my earthly
enemies & persecutors,' but he also noted that Rogers's
interventions 'at one time had so far influenced the good
Bishop's mind, that he . . . gave me to understand . . . that
I must give up all thoughts of Broxbourn . . .'

He recorded later:

'My anxiety continued to June 4th 1801, when Bishop

Porteous gave me his absolute promise; on the 5th I received institution, &c at Fulham. I was "inducted" on the 6th into "the real, actual & corporeal possession of the Church & parish of Broxbourn" by the Revd. Thomas McCulloch Rector of Wormsley . . .

'While the ringers were expressing their joy for my having been inducted (June 6th), Rogers, on his return from Hertford market, *bottle valiant*, dared to cut some of the bell-ropes; but they were spliced very soon; & he, poor wretch, suffered very severely for his folly by being disturbed that whole night, & many succeeding days & nights, not only by the ringing, but by the hissings, hootings & various insults of the populace, who received various sums of money from my parishioners to encourage them in the continuance of their mad frolics & harassings of my *arch-fiend*, Rogers, who was universally detested . . .'

Three months later he wrote:

'Monday Sepr. 7th. Blessed be Heaven! I now enjoy what my soul has long wished for, a considerable share of otium — time at my own disposal. Let it be my constant endeavour to enjoy it cum dignitate. . . . To God alone I owe my present happiness! . . . I know not what envy means. I know not the human being with whom I would exchange situation!!'

His new situation resulted in new resolutions. He noted:

'Dec. 8th. 1801. Left off snuff & hope I shall never return to the *filthy*, worse than *beastly*, practice! . . . O that my *deary* would give up *snuff* & *novels*!!'

By 1802 he was back on snuff, but still revelling in his luck:

'Sunday, Nov. 14th 1802. Broxbourn was my first & only curacy. The good Bishop of London, in whose gift the Living is, cannot, I am sure conceive half of the happiness he has conferred on me, by making me the vicar of the parish. . . . I feel as if my pleasure daily increased . . .'

Early in 1803 he noted:

'Wedy. Jany. 6th. How happy, how very happy, do I feel myself in my dear little room, which some delicate folks would, perhaps, rudely call a *hog-stye*! I am undisturbed. I have my cheerful little fire, my books & in short every comfort which I can reasonably desire. I read. I reflect, I write & . . . enjoy . . . that . . . leisure & absence of care with which Providence . . . has indulged me . . .'

He noted one slight flaw in his enjoyment soon afterwards:

'Wedy. Jany. 26th. I am confident that I am *defrauded* by many of my parishioners of various vicarial dues & rights, to which the laws of Heaven & earth entitled me; but (as I have honestly told some whom it concerned), it is at their *own* peril they do this. And mine is by no means a singular case; for the word "tithe" has ever been unpleasing & odious to farmers especially, as "cuckoo" to the married ear. Those who pay them, pay them very partially, & I may add — "grudgingly & of necessity." . . .'

The following day he gave his views on other clergymen:

'Jany. 27th. Surely the life of a clergyman, if his mind be properly disposed, & attuned, & his outward circumstances at all competent, is of all lives the most happy. But how I do pity the poor unfortunate, who enters into an office so solemn, as a mere profession, or business! What up-hill drudgery & how tedious must the several services appear, when not the *heart*, but the *lips* only are engaged! It is to be feared that there are too many of this unhappy sort. Some unwary youths aspire to the profession, as what is styled "a genteel one." To others their friends and relations dictate this, strongly seconding their cruelly unkind suggestions with the immediate possession of a "handsome preferment" from family or friendly patronage. These are your "master-men" who do their duty by proxy, haggling with poor curates, till they can find those who will starve with the fewest symptoms of discontent.

'As to the fine gentlemen themselves, they are far more

anxious to attain the fame of being "excellent shots," giving the "view halloo" well mounted in the field, & being "in at the death" — than raising their voices in the desk or pulpit . . .

'The sum of this matter appeareth unto me — "he that is despised" as a common servant, or day labourer, & hath the wherewithal to procure the common necessaries of life, is better off than he that *honoureth* himself as a curate & lacketh bread.'

In February incipient money troubles no doubt caused him to philosophise on poverty:

'Feby. 16th. Riches & poverty are, properly speaking, relative terms: but the man who, after discharging every just demand, has a shilling (& still more so, if a guinea), over, may be called a rich man; & he who lacks his guinea, or even shilling, must be content to be numbered among the poor . . .'

Later in the year something of his peace and joy had evaporated:

'Oct. 21st. My little cottage has been quiet, & my hours uninterrupted, for a few, a very few weeks — but I have now a foreigner & a second expected. My *dear* wife seems miserable without them. . . . Would to Heaven I could do without them. It is a severe tax I pay for having a large family, & I lament it more than any other of the lamentable taxes, which are the lot of modern times.'

He was frequently guilty of inserting such sarcastic or plaintive comments about his wife, and himself realised he was overdoing it for in October 1804 he wrote:

'Oct. 1st. I, W.J., the writer of too frequent "domestic Lamentations" am neither more nor less than a *paradox*!

'A stranger who . . . read some of these *dolorous* scrawls, would imagine me to be one of the most miserable of all . . . unhappy beings — but is it so? no — no such thing.'

In 1805 he mentioned his sleeping habits:

'Sep. 22nd. . . . For a considerable time past I have

seldom slept above six hours each night, & many nights not more than five; & I uniformly feel myself the more cheerful throughout the day, the earlier I start in the morning . . . I find my head more clear, & my thoughts more composed for writing, or application of any sort, in the early morning than in the hours that follow the bustle & tumult of the day.

'Oct. 15th.. Often do I, in the dark, by means of holes in the frames of my slates, and moveable pegs, scribble my dawning morning thoughts, a part perhaps of my next Sunday's address; & unless I revise & enter my scrbblements as soon as I get up, they puzzle me as much to decipher them, as Egyptian hieroglyphics can do a poor, rusty antiquarian!'

Later in the year he recorded one occasion when he failed to rise as early as he had intended:

'Dec. 11th. I went to bed about 10 o'clock last night, & when awaked between 12 & 1, by my noisy family's going to bed, I felt as if I had slept sufficiently. I however took another nap, & unclosed my eyes about 5 o'clock, when I seemed resolved to get up; but the morning was so dark & cold that ¼ of my reverend person which was enjoying the warmth of the bed, outpleaded the ¾ which had quitted it, & down I slunk again, like an old hare, into my form; to my shame I did not get up till 8.'

Early in 1806 he expatiated on the evils of some marriages:

'Feby. 8th 1806. In most modern courtships, I believe, the mind has little if any concern. They marry without feeling anything that deserves to be called by the sacred name of love; but alas! they too soon find that they cannot live together without feeling something very much like the *opposite* of love. . . . My friend Du bois is linked with a *Tartar*, a *dogess*, a *tyranness*!! Charles says he often expresses his pity for *me*. Poor fellow! *our mutual pity is unavailing!*'

In February of 1807 he wrote on wine:

'Feby. 4th. Wine &c. Most men know when they had had too little wine, especially since Mr Pitt has *poisoned* — *alias* — highly taxed wine; but if it be poisoned, the less the better we have of it, & I ought to rejoice that my health is not liable to be much that hurt by poisoned wine, at least in my own house. Too many men know, when they have had too much; & I am sorry to add that sometimes, nay too often — this has been my case. But how very much to be regretted that few of us knowing mortals, know when we have had wine enough . . .'

In July, to his great grief, his favourite daughter, Caroline, died after a painful illness. Some idea of the cat-and-dog life he and his wife led may be gathered from her advice to her parents on her deathbed, which he quoted: ' . . . Don't quarrel together! You *might* be very happy! . . . May Heaven give us grace to hearken unto her repeated counsel!' It seems as if this tragedy had the effect of mellowing their relationship, for thereafter his wife is mentioned in much more kindly terms.

An indication of the life of self-denial to which he had accustomed himself, however, is apparent from an entry in November 1807, when Mr William Christie, a local brewer and banker, presented him with £10 to buy: 'no less than a gown, cassock, & the whole *paraphernalia* of a parson! He added a *hat* likewise!' He added:

'When I told the generous man that the between-two-and-three years old hat, which I had worn for some months, on account of it having the crepe for my dear daughter sewed to it, was not the hat, which I had in my study, almost *spick & span* new, tucked up with silver-paper, in a safe & snug box — his reply was — "Never mind, Mr. Jones! get the hat likewise. Store is no sore!" The adage has so much force & truth in it, that I will not attempt to resist it.'

The following day, typically, he had grave doubts:

'Nov. 21st 1807. . . . my very first morning thoughts were occupied by my finery — "that is to be."

'Now if this is not vanity, I shall be glad to be told what it is. And yet I own, that I very much wish to trace my feelings . . . to gratitude, or almost any principle, but that *scurvy, disgusting* one, — vanity; for this would impeach my wife's insight into human characters, she having often told me that she never knew any man so perfectly devoid of vanity as myself! As she and I have been on a very intimate footing for more than 26 years, & I cannot accuse her of flattering her humble servant of a husband; I own that I feel not the least inclination to weaken — much less to annul, her verdict, which *in this instance*, is so favourable to me.

' . . . My old gown is indeed fairly worn out; for it is the selfsame gown, which I wore daily about the streets of Oxford, 27, or more, years ago. My cassock, being made of less durable materials, has long been torn up . . . but having a large family & very limited means, I thought it imprudent to lay out twelve pounds or guineas for new canonicals . . .'

At the end of the month he went up to town and noted:

'Monday Novr. 30th. . . . I returned from Town on Saturday. after throwing away six days there, for I scarce felt the meaning of the word comfort any day except that which I passed in the company of my friends, the Harrisons! 'Twas misery to hear the wretched Londoners wheezing & coughing & gasping for breath, as they walked the streets; & I myself was a fellow-sufferer for fogs & damps, & night-air by no means suit my lungs . . .

'I sometimes think I shall never again spend another week in Town, unless I can contrive to carry my little Study, — my *hutch* with me, as Snails do their shells on their backs.

'But where shall I look for any thing like that watchful & cheerful attention, which my dear girls, Mary & Ellen, shew me? it cannot be purchased . . .'

In 1808 he decided yet again to give up snuff:

'April 28th. I attempted, some years ago, to leave off vile snuff. . . . I am now repeating the same attempt, though I have not entirely discontinued the nasty indulgence . . . my poor nose is very unwilling to be *weaned* . . . (it is a sort of "forlorn hope!") I cannot but be convinced how difficult it is to cast off old habits, however filthy and disgusting!'

He also decided to give up spirits and duly noted:

'July 30th. Smoking & snuff I have (I trust) relinquished, — after the practice of these filthy habits for many years; shall I have the happiness of another, still more desirable conquest? . . .

'But as I have sometimes told my poor nose "I do not mean to *starve* you entirely, or even to *wean* you abruptly; you shall, now & then, be indulged with a *pinch* or *smell* at a box!" even so I may say to my palate "I am invited out to dinner every 2 or 3 months; and then you shall be reminded of the taste or *smatch* of wine &c. & of its undesirable consequences — broken, unquiet slumbers, & to wake with body & mind disturbed & discomposed."'

Early in 1809 he was congratulating himself on his lot compared with that of businessmen of his acquaintance:

'Jany. 14th. 1809. I drank tea at Mr. Cathrow's this evening, (Saty. — a bustling day) with him & his partner, Mr. Christie. I never feel so contented with my own humble lot, as when I mix, now & then, with men of *business*: — & the more they have to do with this world, the less I envy them!'

By September that year, however, he was writing:

'Sept. 1st 1809. Though my wife often reminds me that I could not have *this & that*, without foreigners, & now & then, threatens to put me on coarse fare & short allowances, when we have none of these inmates; yet I cannot help thinking. . . . If the taking of boarders enlarges my *income*, it most certainly curtails my *comforts*.

'My wife & daughters like *bustle*; it keeps their life from stagnating. But I trust the time will come, when they, or my wife at least, will prefer tranquillity & repose . . .'

There came increasingly long gaps marked by such entries as:

'July 13th. 1814. From Sept 15th 1809 to the above date, what a chasm . . .'

In 1816 he noted: 'I do not intend to continue in the profession of teaching much longer.' By this time it would seem that with various deaths amongst their children, as well as with increasing age, both Jones and his wife had begun to mellow, for his comments about her from this point onwards are clearly more affectionate. Yet he was still capable of strong feelings, which he could record firmly enough as for instance:

'Sept. 26th. 1816. . . . I will frankly write what I feel to be the *truth* — that I would infinitely rather receive as guests in my cottage such characters as *publicans & harlots*, if penitent, & brought to a right mind, than any of the prim, formal, & sour-hearted Pharisees who "trust in themselves that they are righteous & despise others." "God declares His almighty power chiefly in showing mercy & pity" — why should any mortal delight in crushing & trampling on a fellow mortal who has fallen?'

He also retained his strong feelings about self-styled gentlemen:

'Oct. 1st 1816. "*Gemmen*" Ought I to wish that it were in my power to furnish my sons with 5 or 600£ a year each? I "trow" not; for it would probably transform them into "*gemmen*" — *alias* — idle, useless & worthless beings.'

On discussion in the Church he wrote equally feelingly:

'Decr. 19th 1816. Sectaries &c. Mr. Miller, the vicar of Harlow Essex, who is a very mild benevolent man, is I am told, often seen "arm in arm" with the dissenting Minister, who is settled in his Parish. I have also been not a little pleased to hear that Dr. Luscombe . . . is intimate with Mr. Maslen, who preached in the "schism-shop" at Hertford. The *hue & cry* is — "The Church is in Danger."

'Let the Ministers of "the Church" shew Christian kindness to Dissenters; if they are obdurate, such conduct will melt them down. If they have any *gall*, this will extract it. If they are at all malicious this will disarm their malice.'

By this time in his sixties, with his grandchildren around him, he noted sadly:

'April 4th 1817. . . . I . . . cannot remark any one house tenanted by the same mortals with whom I conversed thirty-six years ago. Most of the houses have frequently changed their tenants. The houses, gardens, grounds &c., have been, to their utmost "capability," improved and beautified; — & then Death has, without ceremony, or much previous notice, ejected the occupiers. . . . I am almost become a stranger in my own parish . . .'

Yet he could still laugh at himself:

'July 7th 1817. . . . While I am shaving myself, I some-times look into my almost *untoothed* mouth; &, at the same time, consider my various other infirmities, which render me not unlike to a "broken vessel." I thank Heaven that I am not dispirited; my "spirit" bears me up under all my "infirmities;" it is not "wounded" by them.'

Although he still had four years to live it is evident that towards the end of 1817 he had thoughts of approaching death. He wrote:

'Nov. 21st. Dulce domum. I feel that I can neither live nor die anywhere, so comfortably, as in my own nest. I must not attempt to fly far from it. I am often much inconvenienced when only a few hours, or a few miles from my home. I shall very much like to have my *old Mate* & my dear children, around my death-bed. and to utter a few (novissima verba) last words of farewell to them . . .'

A final entry typified the man:

'July 17th 1821. . . . I awoke, not many minutes ago, with my mind under the most pleasing impressions arising from a reliance upon the care of Divine Providence. I am in my bed — with my slate in my hand — but I am unable to transfer to my slate the feelings of my mind.

'Away with all my *worldly* hopes & fears. Away with all my silly plannings & schemings. "My times," & all my concerns, "are in Thy hands," O! my God! *Thy will — not mine — be done! Amen.'*

He died peacefully on 12th October 1821, just a few weeks prior to his sixty-seventh birthday. In his funeral sermon, his friend, the Rev. James Tomlin, spoke of him as one who 'boldly rebuked vice, and patiently submitted to all the insults and indignities which his fidelity might provoke. But he also spake the truth in love so that none could justly take offence.' His wife, Theodosia, died six years later on April 19th, 1827 in her sixty-eighth year and was also buried at Broxbourne. In his diary William Jones still survives, a rare, if sometimes henpecked, spirit.

# 9

## The Rev. Benjamin Newton

### Squarson of Wath: Yorkshire

*Hunting with Lord Darlington . . . Weaned my filly*

Benjamin Newton (1762-1830), son of the vicar of Sandhurst in Gloucestershire, went to Jesus College, Cambridge,
becoming an M.A. in 1786. Subsequently tutor to the
young Lord Ailesbury, he went on to be pluralist holder of
livings in Wiltshire and Somerset, until presented with the
living of Wath in 1814, thanks to the patronage of his erstwhile pupil. The small village of Wath, some four miles
north of Ripon, was in the centre of Lord Ailesbury's Yorkshire estates. It was a rich plum for the incumbent and
provided him with an income of some £700 per annum.

His diary begins with a clear outline of his intentions in
writing it and a good word picture of the diarist himself:

'As I mean this diary to be in some sort a register of my
life, studies and opinions and as I have a great respect for
that heathen precept, Know thyself, I shall make an attempt
to describe myself or in other words to delineate my body
and mind. The former (tho' I have spent as little time as most
men either in the admiration of it or in the cultivating or
adorning of it) I take to have no particular claim to be
thought beautiful, but I bless God that it is in general healthy
and more active and vigorous than the bodies of persons of

*A distant view of the church at Wath showing the tower, built in 1812, the
churchyard and the rectory on the left, from the glebe lands as they were in the
early nineteenth century in the time of the Rev. Benjamin Newton.*

my age (54). . . . I think however it requires considerable attention to keep it in order and health, and that especially without exercise it would soon get unwieldy and consequently inactive and unhealthy. My height is 5ft 9¾ high, my weight about 12 stone, my complexion dark, my head bald, my eyes hazel, and as they tell me quick and bright, not to say sometimes fierce, my nose . . . turned up, my mouth wide and my teeth which were once good very much impaired, my chin round, my neck rather short, my arms and legs rather slender, my gait upright, my body slight inclined to corpulency, my health good, my sleep generally divided into two naps, the first of five hours, the second of two. The only bodily inconvenience I labour under is a great tendency to flatulency, which sometimes disorders my whole system for a time, but is generally of short duration. My mind is generally actively, tho' often I fear not profitably, employed. I am naturally very irritable, but I trust I have in a considerable degree subdued that propensity. My vanity is considerable and I am ashamed of not having made the same conquest of my vanity that I have of my anger. I have in general good spirits, which are seldom depressed except from a sense of my own sins. I have been singularly fortunate and happy thro' life and I think it a duty I owe to God to bear all the little inconveniencies I meet with in patience and gratitude. I have considerable power of application but am nevertheless desultory in my employments.

'I go shooting for health and hunting for society which I like to meet better in the field than at my dinner where I must drink more wine than I like. Of all luxuries I delight most in tea. My appetite is so good I have few predilections. I prefer venison and mutton to all other meat. I like reading, am a great enemy to Tyranny, and greater still to Anarchy. Pitt was too monarchical and Fox too democratical especially during the French Revolution and the Irish Rebellion. My opinion of the Regent I cannot express, his ministers are wicked in nourishing his extravagance. My inclination often leads me to be sarcastic and I am sometimes thought to say a witty thing tho' I did not intend it. I fear I feel too much pleasure in epigram and satyr for a Christian and a Clergyman. I salve my conscience by a conviction that I have no malice. I hate nothing but affectation except downright villainy and sin. I trust I am sufficiently indulgent to my family and servants and too much so to my dogs. I am still charmed with female beauty but rather fastidious in my taste. I am naturally shy but have conquered my shyness by great effort from seeing early the disadvantage of it. I am not a great talker except I think it civil to join or lead the conversation, and I think I can acquit myself of having ever started a subject with the idea of shewing myself off though a sudden impulse makes me shoot a bolt. I seldom or ever tell stories, even short ones. My friends seem fond of my society, rate me much too high. I have studied much to find my own fort. I think it is a sort of power of eliciting fun and wit from the conversation of others rather than from anything of my own "exers ipse secundo." My religious opinions I display at least once a week to my parishioners and therefore have no occasion to record them here. I dread controversy which makes a shipwreck of charity and I see no good in publishing my opinions which are not articles of the Apostle's Creed. As for the Bible Societies, Christian Knowledge Societies, etc., I think it better to pray for one fold under one shepherd leaving the time and the means to the good Shepherd himself to accomplish.'

After this candid summary the diary starts with a visit to Bath in July 1816. In September he returned north, noting:

'September 14th. . . . Arrived at Wath. . . . My farm in good order and my cattle all looking capitally. Found oats and wheat cut . . .'

'15th. Preached at Wath and read prayers in the evening. N.B. A water closet and granary built in my absence, water closet finished.'

He very soon recorded one of the frequent periodic visits

of an old clerical friend of his from his Cambridge days, the Rev. Jacob Costabadie, rector of Wensley-cum-Leyburn, accompanied, as usual, by some of his eleven offspring. They attended the Ripon Ball in early October and Newton later attended the Bedale Agricultural Meeting, where 'forty fine fellows . . . talked of beef and ate pudding and drank wine like trueborn Britons'.

By the end of the first fortnight in October he was shooting and noted:

'15th and 16th. Finished oat, barley and wheat harvest . . .'

On the 20th of October he reflected in his diary:

'In the review of Tweddell's Remains, where it said that out of religious motives he refrained from animal food, it struck me that were this practice to become general, instead of benefitting the species it meant to protect it would lead to their total extinction, in a few years we should have neither sheep, swine, oxen, poultry or game any more than wolves in this country, as the cultivators of grain would then look on all of these species as spoilers and depredators of their crops. Therefore abstinence from animal food seems contrary to reason and Scripture . . .'

He was soon hunting and recorded:

'November 1st. Went hunting to Thornbrugh, found a fox at Norton, had a sharp run for about an hour. Sold my horse Benjamin to Mr. G. Lane Fox who I saw next day at Pickhill where they found a fox. He gave me a letter covering a draft expressive of his satisfaction at the horse, which he told me he had ridden that morning 19 miles in an hour and a quarter and I have since heard that he broke his back at Boro'bridge on his return.'

He paid a return visit to the Costabadies at Wensley and it snowed heavily during his absence. On his return he noted on Sunday the 10th of November:

'Did duty morning and evening. . . . A score of Scots wethers came from Mr. Hunton in my absence. . . . Desired

Costabadie to order me a pipe of port from Hull. Price he thinks about £95. Poor Clarkson's wife died in my absence Tuesday and was buried Thursday. The passage made to the water closet but no roof put yet . . .'

With occasional duties as Justice of the Peace, with further hunting, with his farming and social round, as well as his parish work and clerical duties, his time was fully occupied. In December he recorded:

'December 17th. . . . This being my tithe day I was well satisfied with the result, the whole except £96 being paid, and of that I received £37, so that now the arrears are £59. Walked shooting Monday with J.F. and lost my seals between York Gate and home in the fields.

'18th. Rode to Ripon, carried the money I received yesterday to Coates, £676.'

At the end of the year he wrote:

'30th. Mrs Costabadie and Mary and Charlotte came to Wath . . .

'31st. Ripon Ball.

'January 1st 1817. The Costabadies left us very much pleased with their last night's ball, which was a very good one, 19 couples.'

Some consecutive entries in January indicate the variety of his life:

'17th. Dined at Captain Dalton's with the Oxley's, Askwithe and Col. Dalbiac.

'19th. Did duty morning and evening.

'20th. Ripon Book Club all the members present except Mr. Allanson and Mr. Wood.

'21st. Granted a warrant to apprehend wood stealers from Helflet Wood, (Lord A's).

'23rd. Went hunting with Mr. Bell's hounds . . .'

He was a member of more than one book club, for he noted at the end of the month:

'29th. The Bedale Club. 13 members present . . . determined to have no more auctions but each member should pay ½ a guinea and take the books he ordered at ¼ price and that if any book should be enquired for and not found to be in the room on a club day a bottle of wine should be forfeited to the club and charged to the person in whose possession it was found.'

He was a penetrating critic, as instanced by his comments on Lord Chesterfield's much praised 'Letters':

'13th Feb. . . . Read Lord Chesterfield's letters to his Godson in which I see nothing to admire but the gentlemanly style but his lax morality is shocking to every serious thinking man.'

The following day he recorded, without comment:

'14th. Attended the meeting to enroll the Militia. Little Militia but some Justice business done and we were told of a girl at Burneston who would have been brought to filiate a child she was big with by her own father, but her being brought to bed that morning prevented it . . .'

Early in March he philosophised:

'8th. I trust I may be able to follow the maxim I here lay down as I am convinced of its prudence and propriety and that it is highly conducive to happiness. Never impart a secret to any person but for the purpose of obtaining his assistance or advice on the point of secrecy. The greatest part of what are called secrets are imparted merely because the imparter cannot contain them any longer, possibly a slight gratification may be intended for the hearer but the delivery of himself is the grand object of the labour . . .'

Newton played whist quite often, but it may possibly be inferred from the following entry that he did not like losing:

'5th June. . . . Mr. John Tweedy arrived at Wath and dined and next day brought a friend, a young Mr. Swan, I suppose for a foil as Tweedy is an agreeable, unaffected, well informed young man and Swan is one of the greatest puppies I have met with in a long time. I played four or five rubbers and lost about ten shillings.'

His comments on social aspirations were biting:

'July 19th. Heard Mr. Powlett would not go to any place to dine where Mr Claridge was invited because he was a steward, how soon Mr Powlett seems to have forgotten that he is the son of Orde a country attorney, however this might be of some use to Miss C to know when she is great and grand and teach her that in the scale of society and in the opinion of it too she is below the children of those whose profession the greatest man in the land cannot object merely on the profession's account I make this remark from the high hand with which she seems to carry herself towards the Costabadies, never having seen breezes of that sort towards my girls . . .'

He attended a confirmation service at Jervaux Abbey in August:

'August 10th. Did duty morning and evening and went to dine at Jervaux with the Bishop and two Miss Monsons who carried me to Bedale at night and gave me a bed that I might be ready to meet the Bishop. — [on the]

'11th this morning who breakfasted there, confirmed 984 of which 40 were my parishioners, after the Confirmation the Bishop ascended the pulpit and gave the young people a most appropriate and excellent address. This Confirmation was far better conducted with more regular decency and quiet than I ever saw it before, for which Mr. Monson deserved very great praise, particularly for having carpeted the Church to take off the noise of the country people's hobnails against the flagstones. I returned after having dined with the Bishop . . . well convinced of his being a very good Bishop both in the Church and out of the Church, a conscientious and very agreeable man.'

His comments on people he met were by no means always as favourable and were often acidly illuminating.

'October 22nd. Bedale Club. Present Mr. Scott, a new member, late Chaplain to Lord Nelson, who died aboard the Victory in his arms. He appears a gentlemanly man who has seen much of the world, but seems to have an idea that he is sent here to inform the natives. Dr. Dodsworth who ate an enormous dinner for an octogenarian. Mr. Monson . . .'

He enjoyed varied sporting activities to the full:

'4th November. Coursing on my farm with Mr. Morley, coursed four hares and killed one. I forgot to mention that I killed the first partridge I have killed this year yesterday. Morley afterwards killed a fox at Tanfield . . .

'10th. Hunting with Lord Darlington at Baldersby Cundall. Weaned my filly, sent six sheep bought at Middleham to Mr. Morley. Hired Mrs Humphrie's brother to come in Will Houseman's place, at £7 if he behaves himself and 6 guineas if he is not obedient.'

Servants could be a source of domestic friction as he noted:

'2nd December. . . . had a long discussion about Charlotte Barnett from which I am more than ever convinced that the moment any servant becomes such a favourite with Master or Mistress that the one cannot find fault without offending or shocking the feelings of the other, that is the moment when the servant should be discharged. For to mark the progress of this discussion whether I am right or wrong in the view of Charlotte's behaviour, when the dog barked my wife rang the bell and no one answered and I immediately said Charlotte had left the house and gone to the junketting, she flatly contradicted me, rang again, and at last got up not from any fear that the house was left open to robbers but for the purpose of confuting my uncharitable charge upon her favourite. She is not afraid of robbers nor ever was. After she had searched the house and could only find C was gone out . . . she returned to bed, she could not close her eyes even after all the servants were returned but because I expressed my displeasure at the conduct of the favourite. And tho' till the moment she detected her she considered the breach of confidence reposed in her so heinous that she could not be guilty of it, as soon as she was convinced that she had gone to the dance, instead of entering into all my feelings in the subject she set herself to find out excuses and palliations and to make me think as well of her as before, tho' if I had told Henry that I had given all the rest of the servants leave to go and desired him to stay and take charge of the house and he had undertaken it as she did and left it as she did, he should never have entered it again. Yet I am told because I say I can't think as well of her as before that I am very uncharitable and all the girls with more zeal than either wisdom or duty are drawn to support this system of favouritism of their mother. . . . So much for favourite servants, the best fuel in the world to light a fire of family discord.'

Less than three weeks later he noted:

'22nd. . . . Perceived Charlotte to be getting very big again . . .'

Newton's son, the Rev. John Farmer Newton had some years previously married an heiress, Elizabeth Kent, with whom he had fallen in love while still at College. Subsequently the young couple had lived extravagantly and ended in financial difficulties resulting in an estrangement the previous year. By this time reconciled, J.F. Newton and his wife and baby son were staying at Wath prior to his ordination and taking up his father's perpetual curacy at Biddisham in Somerset. It is clear that Newton viewed his son and daughter-in-law with some amusement and enjoyed their company. He wrote:

'6th March 1818. Went hunting with Boro'bridge hounds and had great sport. Mr. Claridge called yesterday and took away his daughter who had been flirting for three weeks with J.F.N in such a way as to make Mrs J.F.N dislike her exceedingly and my wife vows she will never ask her to stay again when J.F.N is in the house. She assumed the character of Lady Grave-airs for a time, but though she said she thought a quiet manner the most interesting, hoyden came uppermost at least ten times a day. The sooner she is married to prevent her laying in the hedge the better. Eliza's manner was quite perfect with her. I think her more agreeable every day. . . . Her wit is so playful that it cuts blocks like a razor tho' the blocks are insensible of the gashes tho' they are very deep. Dr. Whaley has called more than once and I find his sitting breeches stick closer to chairs than ever . . .'

The following day he wrote on the death of his dog:

'7th. . . . I have to record the loss of an old and faithful friend in my little dog Pam who was unfortunately killed by my son's horse laying upon him in the stable where he was sent to dry himself after having been washed and was forgotten to be taken into the house again at night. He was 12 years old, very sagacious and affectionate, particularly handsome and never had any descendants at all equal to him in beauty. For many years he slept in our room. He was of a very amiable disposition and had as far as I am able to judge no evil propensity. He was grave but could be gay. Interpreter not only of looks and actions, but often I thought of words also. He remembered his friends at any distance of time and expressed himself with pleasure at seeing them after a long or a short absence.'

When his daughter suffered what sounds like pneumonia, he noted:

'19th March. Rode to Pickhill with Anne and Mrs Newton and the former this morning (20th) complained of a violent shivering before we went to Church and which made her sisters prevail upon her not to go, on coming from Church (where J.F.N read prayers and I preached and administered the Sacraments) we found her alarmingly ill and immediately sent for Dr. Whaley who gave her a dose of calomel with salts and senna which however seemed to yield no relief to her head which continued most excruciating and she was scarcely anything relieved this morning (21st) when three leches applied to her temples seemed to give slight relief. Dr. Whaley came at one and applied eight more which seem to take off the pain from her head but a large blister was applied to the nape of the neck which reached down between her shoulders she is left this morning (22nd) much exhausted from want of sleep and much evacuation . . .

'22nd Easter Sunday. J.F.N read prayers and I preached and administered the Sacraments. . . . I had the happiness of hearing on my return from Church that my dear Anne was more improved than Dr. Whaley could have expected . . .'

Despite the doctor she was on the way to recovery two days later and Newton took his son and daughter-in-law dancing and racing as he recorded:

'24th. Ripon Ball with J.F.N, Eliza. . . . Sold two cows at Bedale Fair for £30.9.0.

'25th. To Bedale with J.F.N, Eliza . . . and from thence to Richmond.

'26th. Thence to Catterick Races. . . . Had good sport at the Races and were highly gratified at seeing Mr Claridge's horse win the Produce Stakes. . . . Returned to Wath about nine . . .

'29th. . . . My dear Anne left her room for the first time today. I bless God for her recovery.'

He was very much a family man and later wrote:

'15th June. This was a melancholy week as my dear children and grandson were to leave us at the end. I hope yet to have them established at no great distance of time in the neighbourhood before I am quite over the hill and unable to enjoy their society. I trust my behaviour to them during their visit will prevent them ever gain mistaking my motives of action towards them. I gave J.F.N a discharge of all monies due to me previous to 1st January last, to my belief about £400 and lent him £85 for which he gave me his note of hand 'to his three sisters and a promise to pay it as soon as he could and at all events on the marriage of either. I also promised to give up all the profits of Biddisham and to try to get it resigned to him, only that I am not to pay curate since Christmas last or to stand repairs, but I gave up all arrears after paying curate up to Christmas last and the business of the Priory is for ever set at rest between us . . .

'16th. Dined with my wife and J.F.N and Eliza at Morley's who gave us a most splendid dinner and won our money afterwards.

'22nd. . . . This day J.F.N, Eliza and dear Jack . . . left Wath.'

In July he noted:

'3rd July. Heard from Mr. Claridge that he had bought Lord Ashton's barouch for me for £140 including a new boot and painting the crest.

'27th. . . . Played chess with Mr. Assey who beat me very much, I attribute it to playing with the red men, instead of the white to which I am most accustomed . . .

'28th. Played at chess again with Mr. Assey and beat him pretty easily with the white men . . .'

In September there arose a contretemps between his old friend Costabadie and Lord Ailesbury's agent, Mr Claridge. He noted:

'13th. Did duty morning and evening . . . In the evening received a basket of game, four partridges and a hare from Mr. Claridge and a packet of correspondence on the subject of Costabadie having gone shooting on Lord Ailesbury's land near Jervaux. I am sorry for it as Costabadie will be very much annoyed and a forbidding to shoot is always a closing of intercourse between the forbidder and the forbidden and I am pretty sure this case will not prove an exception. I was very sorry also on Mr. Claridge's account as it is confirmation of what I have heard urged against Mr. C. whenever almost his name has been brought up, viz: there is no certainty in an agent, he is Mr. Claridge as long as it suits his purpose to associate with the gentlemen of the country, but when it suits his purpose he is then only Lord A's agent or steward. No one believes that Lord A would refuse anyone liberty to shoot that Mr. Claridge would approve and everyone believes that when any person is referred for

leave by Mr Claridge to Lord A or by Lord A to Mr Claridge
that the answer he will receive has been prearranged
between them; and if it were not so there could not exist that
excellent understanding between them which does exist.
Powlett's saying he would not sit down with C because he
was a steward was one of the greatest pieces of impudence
that ever came out of the mouth of the son of a country
attorney . . .'

Newton supported his old friend and wrote:

'16th. . . . Received a letter . . . from Mr Claridge on the
subject of Costabadie. I find by his letter that Mr Scrope has
the deputation of the manor where C was shooting. This in
my present idea makes Mr. Claridge's interference more
improper as to the forbidding. The first note was all that
ought to have been sent and especially until it was certain
that it had been received. Mr. Claridge's reply to me is
shifting his ground. His first letter to me was not, as I
apprehended, to ask me whether Costabadie had done
wrong but whether he himself had done right. Costabadie
admits he had not done right and Mr Claridge makes no
reply to my argument about the main point which was C's
veracity.'

Clearly, knowing Newton was a friend of Lord Ailesbury
and of Costabadie, the agent had hoped to justify himself,
but Costabadie does not seem to have been unduly worried
as Newton noted in October:

'1st. . . . Letter from . . . Costabadie who takes no notice
of what has passed between him and Mr Claridge . . .'

Like many other clergymen Newton often pointed his
sermons with an eye to their effect on his parishioners and
he noted:

'17th October. . . . Was much pleased to hear that Mrs.
Askwith with her husband's permission invited Mr and Mrs
Dawson to their ball which is to be given on Wednesday and
felt very severe pleasure in the idea that what I had glided
into my last Sunday's sermon purposely to touch Mr A had

some effect. I was well aware it was a very delicate and difficult point to handle. Anything direct or abrupt would have defeated its own purpose and it was no easy matter to touch him without being apparently personal or appearing so either to him or others. The text however was such as could not alarm him or give suspicion and I rejoice he made the application which I fully intended he should to himself of that which was conveyed in the most general terms I could avail myself of. I was again gratified by the way Mrs Harrison said to me at Ripon when speaking of Mr Askwith's intended ball "And the Dawsons are to be there.'

That his reading tastes were varied and his criticisms trenchant may be judged from an entry two days later:

'19th October. . . . Rode to Ripon . . . went to the Book Club . . . order Woman, or *Pour et Contre*, Hogg's Brownie, Birbeck's Notes on America, Jones's History of the Peninsular War, Rosive's Life of Lorenzo de Medici, Richard's Sermon on the Poor Laws. . . . Read Eustace's Tour and think he is the best dissenter I have met with, rather prolix about the Churches, especially such as have nothing at all extraordinary about them. Finished the last Tales of My Landlord of which the fourth volume is the worst. I think Walter Scott has the peculiar art of growing worse and worse and yet preserving his popularity. One poem after another was worse than the former, just as his Tales and every volume of every Tale continues in a similar climax of deterioration.'

Hunting once again in November he noted:

'21st. . . . There was one of the largest and most gentlemenly fields I ever saw . . .'

In December he wrote:

'7th. Went hunting. . . . Sold my young mare for 25 guineas to Mr Dent who tried to buy her for 22 at Topcliffe Fair . . .'

His final entry in December indicated that he did his share financially as well as morally for his parishioners but also ended on a rather different, more personal, note:

'27th. Did duty morning and evening. . . . Gave away the Poor and Sacrament money amounting to £37 and added about two guineas, which with the blankets bought at Home's makes up about five pounds and with ten for the doctoring, ten for the schooling at Heldridge, ten for Bibles and puddings at home, makes up the principal parts of my donation to the poor of Wath. . . . Wrote to Mr Claridge and offered £15 for the Bishop of Chester's mare. . . . The frost and rhyme went off without rain. Beans and peas look well, gathered roses and July flowers. . . . Sold the old carriage to Williamson for five guineas . . .'

With this characteristic mixture of details regarding his parochial duties, nature notes, horticulture, horse-coping and farming, his diary ends. The social side-light involved in selling his old carriage for £5 when he had recently bought Lord Ashton's for £140 is very typical of his dealings. He must have proved a perfect sporting squarson, that peculiarly eighteenth-century mixture of squire and parson, in a very suitable setting and no doubt his parishioners, sporting Yorkshiremen themselves, fully appreciated him.

# 10

## The Three Sages: Aeneas, Alexander and Donald

### Highland Ministers: Sutherland

*My father sat behind me . . . and groaned aloud from very anxiety*

Donald Sage (1789-1869), who wrote his Memoirs, part autobiographical, part diary, in the nineteenth century, was a Presbyterian minister whose Highland antecedents went back to the early eighteenth century. Himself minister of Strathnaver in 1819 during the last of the notorious Highland Clearances by order of the Duke of Sutherland, he was third in line of a family already notable as Highland ministers. His grandfather, Aeneas Sage, inducted as minister of Lochcarron in 1726, died, still in office, in 1774. His father, Alexander Sage, was minister of Kildonan during the earlier clearance there by the Sutherland family in 1814.

Aeneas Sage was a man of immense stature and strength, initially strongly resented as a 'Whig' southern minister. He was, however, perhaps the right man in the right place, for he was to require all his muscle to subdue some of his parishioners, who would accept no other form of authority. Donald Sage wrote:

'The early years of my grandfather's ministry were . . . very disheartening. The parishioners with the exception of one or two families refused to attend his ministry; and not

*A sheep grazing in the ruins of the township of Grumbeg, above Loch Naver, at the head of Strath Naver, scene of part of the infamous Sutherland Clearance of 1819, when over 1,600 people were evicted to make way for sheep, as recorded by the Rev. Donald Sage at the time.*

content with this negative opposition, the more desperate characters among them attacked him violently. After his settlement, to show their dislike, the people assembled every Lord's day in a plot of ground about twenty yards from the church door for the practice of athletic games . . .'

The reasons for this behaviour stemmed from the strong antagonism between Highlands and Lowlands that had developed during the seventeenth century. With the Union of the Crowns in 1603 the Lowland Scots no longer felt the need for the Highland military strength to call on as armed reserves in time of need. The success of Montrose's brilliant but brief campaign in support of Charles I, which ended in 1645 with the Lowlands completely at the mercy of a Highland force, generated the seeds of fear and mistrust already latent in Lowland minds. The subsequent actions of the government in the south culminating in the notorious Massacre of Glencoe in 1692 aroused similar fear and mistrust in Highland minds.

The Highland way of life, which had remained virtually unchanged for centuries, was an anachronism in a rapidly changing world. The methods first adopted by James VI and I in 1609 for undermining the clan system by insisting on education in English rather than Gaelic had been greatly extended by the end of the century, if still largely ineffectual. Amongst the Acts introduced by William III were measures 'for rooting out the Erse language and for other *pious* uses'. The Society for the Propagation of Christian Knowledge was formed with missionary zeal to send Lowland ministers to Highland parishes with a view to converting the supposedly 'heathen' Highlanders. Not unnaturally the 'Whig' ministers, as they were generally termed, speaking for the most part only English, had an uphill task, being regarded as southern interlopers.

In Aeneas Sage's case he eventually made a bargain with one of his parishioners that if he would attend church every Sunday he would reward him with a pound of snuff. Donald

Sage continued:

'The agreement was made and for the space of nearly a year was scrupulously acted on by the minister and the parishioner. The minister regularly preached, the parishioner as regularly heard, and afterwards duly received his modicum of snuff. The poor man's hour came at last. My grandfather had preached a sermon from these words: "What shall it profit a man should, etc." When he thereafter went up to his pensioned hearer and reached out to him his usual allowance, the poor fellow turned away and burst into tears: "No, sir," said he, "I receive that no longer. Too long have I been hearing God's word for hire, to-day I have heard it to my own condemnation." My grandfather exhorted and encouraged him and he ultimately became one of the best fruits of his ministry.'

Some of Aeneas Sage's methods were more forthright:

'There was a small proprietor in the parish who was known to be a libertine . . . one particular Sabbath, Mr Sage . . . intimated his intention to hold a diet of catechising in this man's house. . . . When he arrived . . . on the day appointed, the owner met him at the door, and with a menacing scowl asked, what brought him there? "I come to discharge my duty to God, to your conscience and to my own" was the answer. "I care nothing for any of the three," said the man. "Out of my house — or I'll turn you out." "Easier said than done," said my grandfather. "But you can turn me out if you can." This pithy colloquy brought matters to an issue. They were both powerful men. . . . After a short but fierce struggle the minister became the victor and the landlord . . . was, with a rope coiled round his arms and feet, bound over to keep the peace. The people of the district were then called in, and the minister proceeded seriously to discharge the duty of catechising them. When that was finished he set himself to deal with the delinquents present. The man was solemnly rebuked and the minister so moved his conscience that . . . he and the woman with whom he co-habited . . . [were] duly and regularly married. The man afterwards became a decided Christian.'

It is not surprising that such a rumbustious character, although entirely in keeping with the wild surroundings of Lochcarron, should fall foul of the General Assembly as he did in June 1759, when George Ridpath noted[1] that he was rebuked for his malignant heresy-hunting disposition. It was difficult enough for a Lowlander like George Turnbull to understand the Highlanders in the Trossachs in 1698[2] and just as hard for Ridpath in his snug border parish half a century later. It is very doubtful if Aeneas Sage bothered about such reprimands from Edinburgh. According to Donald Sage:

'He died on the 15th day of July, 1774, in the 88th year of his age and the 48th of his ministry. He appears to have been mentally alert to the very end, and deeply mourned by his family and parishioners on whom he had made a lasting impression.'

Regarding his father (1753-1824) Donald Sage wrote:

'My father, Alexander Sage, minister of Kildonan in Sutherlandshire, my grandfather's sixth son, was born at the manse of Lochcarron on the 2nd of July, 1753. . . . He went to Aberdeen University in 1776. . . . His first appointment was that of parochial schoolmaster of Tongue. . . . As a teacher my father had three distinguishing qualities — assiduity, fidelity and, I must add, severity. The last of these arose from a hasty temper and his own early training. . . . He was six feet one inch in height, with great breadth of chest and shoulders. To his scholars therefore his temper when ruffled was no trifle . . .'

In 1779 Alexander Sage was licensed to preach and sent as assistant to the Rev. Alexander Pope, minister of Reay.

'Mr Pope was settled at Reay in 1734. He was a man of extraordinary strength, fervent piety and unflagging zeal. His parishioners when he first settled among them were not only ignorant but flagrantly vicious. Like the people of

Lochcarron they were Episcopalians in name, but heathens in reality. Mr Pope soon discovered that they required a very rough treatment and being from his strength furnished with a sufficient capacity to administer any needful chastisement, he failed not vigorously to exercise it. He usually carried about with him a short thick cudgel, which from the use he was compelled to make of it . . . was known as "the bailie" . . .' (i.e. magistrate.)

When Mr Pope died in 1782, Alexander Sage was appointed to a mission in Strathalladale. Donald Sage commented:

'Missions . . . were of long standing. . . . The object was to supply the almost total lack of ministerial service in the extensive parishes of the north. . . . Missions were established for the accommodation of such of the parishioners for whom it was a physical impossibility to attend the parish church. For the support of the missionary ministers there were two sources of funds, the Christian Knowledge Society [established by Royal Charter in 1701] and the Assembly's Committee. . . . To send forth ministers, catechists, and schoolmasters . . . was the peculiar province of the Society . . . upon the whole it was very inefficient and . . . is almost defunct.'

In 1787 Alexander Sage was appointed minister of Kildonan in Sutherland. It was there that Donald Sage was born in 1789. In 1804 he went to Aberdeen University, returning to act as parochial schoolmaster at Loth in the summer vacations, until he became a Master of Arts in 1808. He then went on to become schoolmaster at Bower in Caithness. He had little good to say about the ministers there, particularly Mr Smith, the eccentric minister of Bower:

'Mr Smith . . . was both a talented man and an accomplished scholar. But his religion both in the pulpit and out of it, was at the best a mere caprice of the moment. He had, in his public prayers, a volubility and variety of words and expression, and even of ideas, such as they were, which had nothing of the spirit of devotion. No-one could ever have conceived that he was addressing his Creator, but rather that he was exhibiting like a mountebank on the boards of a platform. Then, in his sermons and expository lectures on scripture, he was always straining after something curious, or sarcastic, or puzzling, even profane. There was no unction, no edification, no solemnity, not even sound scripture doctrine, but a sort of nondescript jumble of everything that might be said or fancied on the text, however . . . absurd or contradictory. Then his private devotions, as well as conversations with his people, were equally frivolous and flighty. . . . If any of his parishioners conversed with him on light or secular subjects he changed the subject at once into that of a grave or solemn cast; and if any of them spoke to him about the state of their minds, or the concerns of their souls, he turned the whole at once into a jest.'

Donald Sage described Mr Smith's neighbour in similar terms:

'His co-presbyter, Mr. John Cameron of Halkirk, was his twin brother in levity and folly. . . . Nothing could be more irreverent or unedifying than his appearance in the pulpit. He had a stuttering, rapid utterance, slurring his words so much as to make them unintelligible, or, if they were understood, they were so perfectly ludicrous as often to set his audience a-langhing. He usually read his English sermons. The manuscripts were at least forty years old, the crude lucubrations of his younger years, whilst the deep yellow hue of the leaves, and their tattered and rounded corners bore ocular testimony to their antiquity. He was diminutive in person, had an ill-combed shock of grey hair coming down on his forehead and shoulders, with a countenance strongly expressive of levity, drollery, profanity and folly. He died at the manse of Halkirk on the 8th of Dec. 1822 at the advanced age of 88 . . .'

A contemporary of these, the Rev. Roderick Mackenzie of Knockbain in Beauly, who was appointed in 1790, was also well described:

'In regard to personal appearance, stature and strength, few men in the five northern counties could compete with "Parson Rory" as he was usually called. He was upwards of six feet in height, with broad shoulders and massive, well proportioned limbs. In his younger days he wore the Highland costume and was universally allowed to have been one of the finest looking Highlanders of his day. His features were bold and prominent, approaching to coarseness, and his eye had a twinkle in it strongly indicative of Highland cunning and sagacity. His character as a preacher and minister was much lowered by his . . . habits as a man. . . . The doctrines of the gospel he preached with Calvinistic purity, but in practice he wholly laid them all aside. . . . He was a first-rate shot and deer stalker, the boon companion and fellow sportsman of all comers, English, Irish or Scotch. To do him justice, however, the only symptom of inebriety which he ever showed was to speak somewhat thick and to snivel through his nose. These were the days when drinking was more or less practised at every dinner table. A notorious wine-bibber . . . from England . . . never ceased taunting Kilcoy [one of Roderick Mackenzie's heritors] and the Scotch for their very slender capacity . . . in what he called the manly science of drinking . . . Kilcoy . . . stated his grievance to Parson Rory. "Weell," said the parson, "it would not do to make it public, but if you give us a good dinner I think I'll try him." . . . After dinner, wine-glasses were placed before the sitters at the table. "Away with these trifles," said the Englishman, "and bring us tumblers." The tumblers were brought. "Away with these silly tumblers," said the parson, "and place before this gentleman and me a cup and a bottle of port wine for each of us." The order was obeyed. Parson Rory, decanting the bottle of port into the cup and raising it to his lips, said "Sir, I pledge you" and then, at a single draught, emptied the contents. . . . The Englishman stared and declared himself fairly beaten. The parson felt none the worse of it . . .'

He was very benevolent and particularly attentive to the poor and destitute. His character was accurately described by a shrewd old innkeeper at Contin, who lived during the successive incumbencies of Messrs MacLennan, Mackenzie and Dallas. . . . 'The first we had, sir, was a minister, but he was not a man — a Mr Maclennan; the second, Mr Rory, was a man but no minister; but he we now have is neither a man nor a minister.'

From 1809 to 1813 Donald Sage attended divinity sessions in the winter months; the first six sessions at Aberdeen and the last two at Edinburgh. In 1813 he acted as private tutor for nearly a year, while recuperating from an illness, to the family of Mr MacKid, the Sheriff of Tain. He recorded:

'It was a very short time previous to my residence in Mr. MacKid's family that the first "Sutherland Clearance" took place. This consisted in the ejection from their minutely divided farms of several hundreds of the Sutherland aborigines, who had from time immemorial been in possession of their mountain tenements. This . . . fell most heavily on the parish of Kildonan. It was the device of one William Young . . . [who] introduced the depopulating system into Sutherland. . . . The whole . . . of the Strath from Kildonan to Caen on the left bank of the river and from Dalcharn to Marrel on the right bank, were at one fell swoop cleared of their inhabitant. The measures for their ejectment had been taken with such promptness and were so suddenly and brutally carried out, as to excite a tumult among the people. Young had as his associate in the factorship a man by the name of Sellar . . . who, by his unprincipled recklessness in conducting the process of ejectment, added fuel to the flame. It was said that the people rose almost en masse. . . . But the chief magistrate of the county, shrewdly suspecting the origin of these reports . . . instituted a cool and impartial enquiry. . . . The result was . . . it could not be proved that a single act of violence was committed. Sellar laboured hard to involve my father and mother . . . but he utterly failed. The peasantry, as fine as any in the world, were treated by the owners of the soil as "good for nothing but to be cast out and trodden under the feet of man" while the tract of country thus depopulated was divided into two large sheep-farms . . .'

He noted:

'A vast extent of moorland within the parishes of Farr and Kildonan was let to Mr. Sellar, factor for the Stafford family . . . as a sheep . . . farm: and the measure he employed to eject the poor, but original possessors of the land, was fire. At Rhimisdale, a township crowded with small tenants, a corn-mill was set on fire in order effectually to scare the people from the place before the term for eviction arrived. Firing . . . a corn mill . . . was punishable by imprisonment . . . and on this point of law Mr Sellar was ultimately tried. The Sheriff-substitute Mr R. MacKid . . . considered himself called upon to issue a warrant for Mr Sellar's apprehension and incarceration in Dornoch jail, and to prepare the case for the Inverness Circuit Court. . . . The trial took place, but . . . Sellar was acquitted, while Sheriff MacKid was heavily censured. . . . The whole matter, however, left a stain on the memory of the perpetrators which will never be removed.'

During 1815, while preparing for the ministry, Sage acted as tutor to cousins of his named Mathieson at Lochcarron, where he continued his trials under the Presbytery of Lochcarron. He described the various ministers with his customary candour:

'Mr Lachlan Mackenzie was then minister of Lochcarron. . . . Of all his nine co-presbyters Mr Mackenzie was the only minister who preached the gospel with purity and effect. Mr Morrison of Crow-Kintail adopted the evangelical strain, but was more remarkable for his blundering than for any actual efficiency. Dr Ross of Lochbroom was an able man, and a sound and talented preacher, but his love of controversy and litigation destroyed his ministerial usefulness, and was withering his soul. Mr Downie of Lochalsh was a man of wealth and gentlemanly manners, a princely landlord, and extensive sheep farmer, a good shot, but a wretched preacher. Mr Russel of Gairloch, Mr Macrae of Glenshiel, Mr Macqueen of Applecross and Mr Colin Macivor of Glenelg were complete and respectable specimens of Moderation in those days.'

Later in 1815 Sage was licensed to preach and was appointed to the vacant mission of Achness in Strathnaver, stopping off on his way there at the manse at Kildonan. Surprisingly enough he recorded that at this time he was 'wretchedly deficient in the Gaelic language'. For one who was brought up in the Highlands this was a strange admission and indicative of the fact that schooling was entirely conducted in English. Thus inevitably when it came to preaching both in Gaelic and English he found it difficult to adapt. He noted on his return to Kildonan that his father was preparing for communion services:

'I found my father, with his assistant, Mr John Munro, missionary minister of Dirlot, and Mr Duncan MacGillivray, minister of Assynt busily engaged in the preparatory duties. The services were conducted in Gaelic and in the open air . . . about a mile north of the manse. . . . My father preached the action sermon in Gaelic and I succeeded him in the evening. . . . I uttered a few preliminary sentences with considerable boldness and facility. But all at once my memory failed me and I made a dead pause. My father sat behind me in the tent, and groaned aloud from very anxiety. . . . After a pause of some minutes . . . I pulled out my manuscript and stammered out the rest of my sermon with much trepidation and in the best way I could. I returned home totally disconcerted and seriously meditated the renunciation of my licence, my mission and all my ministerial prospects.'

Despite this setback he was ordained in November 1816 and took up his mission in Achness, which he described:

'The mission . . . was . . . of very great extent. It lay within the bounds of the neighbouring presbyteries of Tongue and Dornoch. . . . A very considerable portion of the population had already been removed by the Stafford family and their tenements given to sheep farmers, so that the peopled part of the district was comparatively limited. The whole population of the Strathnaver district . . . lived . . . in detached townships . . . Mondale, Tobeg, Grummore, Grumbeg, Ceannachyle, Syre, Langdale, Skaill. and Carnachadh — all possessed by small tenants . . . my furniture was scanty, and my books were few. Some articles of furniture I got from the manse at Kildonan . . .'

In October 1818, within two years, he received an eviction order to be out by the following May. He wrote of this last great Sutherland Clearance of 1819:

'. . . my ministry at Achness . . . was drawing fast to its close. The reckless lordly proprietors had resolved upon the expulsion of their long-standing and much-attached tenantry from their widely extended estates, and the Sutherland Clearance of 1819 was not only the climax of their system of oppression . . . but the extinction of the last remnant of the ancient Highland peasantry in the north . . .'

He described the background in some detail:

'It might be about the beginning of October, 1818. . . . Summonses of ejectment were issued and despatched all over the district. These must have amounted to upwards of a thousand, as the population of the Mission alone was 1600 souls, and many more than those of the Mission were ejected. The summonses were distributed with the utmost precision. They were handed in at every house and hovel alike, be the occupiers of them who, or what they might — minister, catechist, or elder, tenant or sub-tenant, out-servant or cottar — all were made to feel the irresponsible power of the proprietor. The enormous amount of citations might also be accounted for by the fact that Mr Peter Sellar had a threefold personal interest in the whole matter. He was, in the first place, factor of the Sutherland estate at the time; then, he was law agent for the proprietors; and, lastly, the lessee, or tacksman of more than a third of the country to be cleared of its inhabitants. It may easily be conceived how such a three plied cord of worldly interest would bind him over to greater rigour and even atrocity, in executing the orders of his superiors on the wretched people among whom he was thus let loose like a beast of prey . . .'

Remembering Sellar's attempts to accuse his father of causing trouble in 1815 no doubt Sage felt inhibited about raising protests. He recorded:

'I could not but regard the summoning of the minister as tantamount to putting down the ministration of the word and ordinances of religion in that part of the country. And . . . although this desolate district is still occupied by shepherds, no provision has since that time been made for their spiritual wants. I left Achness, therefore, about the middle of November 1818, sold my cow at Ardgay market, and got my furniture conveyed to Kildonan by my father's horses and my own.'

He decided, however, to 'continue the punctual discharge of my pastoral duties among the people until they should be moved'. He wrote of his final sermon:

'On Strathnaver we assembled for the last time at the place of Langdale, where I had frequently preached before, on a beautiful green sward. . . . The still-flowing waters of the Naver swept past us a few yards to the eastward. The Sabbath morning was unusually fine, and mountain, hill and dale, water and woodland, among which we had so long dwelt and with which all our associations of 'home and Native-land' were so fondly linked, appeared to unite their attractions to bid us farewell. . . . The service began. The very aspect of the congregation was of itself a sermon, and a most impresive one. Old Achoul sat right opposite me. As my eye fell on his venerable countenance, bearing the impress of eighty seven winters, I was deeply affected and could scarcely articulate the psalm. I preached and the people listened, but every sentence uttered and heard was in opposition to the tide of our natural feelings, which, setting against us, mounted at every step of our progress higher and higher. At last all restraints were compelled to give way. The preacher ceased to speak, the people to listen. All lifted up their voices and wept, mingling their tears together. It was indeed the place of parting and the hour. The greater number parted never again to behold each other in the land of the living . . .'

If only by hearsay, he described the evictions themselves in some detail:

'The middle of the week brought on the day of the Strathnaver Clearance. It was a Tuesday. At an early hour of that day Mr Sellar, accompanied by the Fiscal, and escorted by a strong body of constables, sheriff officers and others, commenced work at Grummore, the first inhabited township to the west of the Achness district. Their plan of operation was to clear the cottages of their inmates, giving them about half an hour to pack up and carry off their furniture, and then set the cottage on fire. To this plan they recklessly adhered, without the slightest regard to any obstacle that might arise while carrying it into execution . . .'

He saw the results the following week and described them thus:

'I had occasion on the week immediately ensuing to visit the manse of Tongue. On my way thither, I passed through the scene of the campaign of burning. The spectacle was hideous and ghastly! The banks of the lake and river, formerly studded with cottages, now met the eye as a scene of desolation. Of all the houses, the thatched roofs were gone; but the walls built of alternate layers of turf and stones remained. The flames of the preceding week still slumbered in their ruins, and sent up into the air spiral columns of smoke; whilst here a gable and there a long side wall undermined by the fire burning within them, might be seen tumbling to the ground, from which a cloud of smoke and then a dusky flame, slowly sprang up . . . nothing could more vividly represent the horrors of grinding oppression and the extent to which one man, dressed up in a "little brief authority" will exercise that power without feeling or restraint to the injury of his fellow-creatures.'

On learning of the eviction of their missionary and his flock, the Assembly of the Church of Scotland raised no protest but simply dissolved the mission and three months later Sage was appointed to the Gaelic Chapel in Aberdeen. Here he remained until 1822, having married in 1821. In May 1822 he was inducted to Resolis on the Black Isle, but to his great grief his wife died in childbirth shortly afterwards. Two years later his father also died at Kildonan, where he had been living since the Clearance of 1814 with no congregation and no parishioners, indeed with no company except the schoolmaster, who was similarly placed.

In 1826 Donald Sage married again and lived happily at Resolis until the Disruption of the Church of 1843, when he joined the Free Church of Scotland. He subsequently noted:

'In looking back on that period of my life when I was a minister of the Establishment, I have good cause to congratulate myself on the exchange. . . . For the twenty years consecutively in which I was a minister of the Established Church I did not receive a farthing of my stipend without a *grudge*, or even without a *curse* of my heritors along with it. The delays they ever made in paying at the term, the insolent and ill grounded excuses they advanced for such delays, and the vexatious litigious disputes into which they led me to enforce payment, were calculated not only to prevent me from laying anything by for the education of my family, and for the necessities of old age, but even to deprive me of the means of payment of my lawful debts, or of procuring the most ordinary necessities of life. . . . How different was all this from, and how very contrary to, the treatment which I have uniformly received since I joined our beloved and truly noble-minded Free Church of Scotland. . . . After shaking myself free of the Establishment and its annoying, unhallowed appendages, and joining the free Church I may truly say that I exchanged debt and poverty for peace of mind and a competency, enabling me to supply my everyday wants and to pay all my debts . . .'

## NOTES

1 See p. 80.
2 See p. 36.

# 11

## The Rev. John Skinner

### Neurotic Antiquarian: Somerset

*I am not to be frightened by the opposition of the lower orders*

The Rev. John Skinner (1772-1839) was ordained in 1799 aged twenty-seven, having first studied for the Bar. He was presented with the living of Camerton by an uncle in 1800 and was thus 'assured . . . a comfortable independence'. Situated about six miles from Bath, coal-mining was the principal industry. In 1805 he married and the following year his favourite daughter, Laura, was born. Owen, his elder son, was born in 1808, his second daughter Anna in 1809 and his younger son, Joseph, in 1810. A third daughter died in infancy in 1811 and his wife died in 1812. Eight years later in 1820 his daughter Laura also died.

Up to this point his Journals had been little more than records of his archaeological investigations. From this point onwards without his wife or favourite daughter to confide in, his diaries to a great extent took their place. A picture of the slowly disintegrating life of the rectory and the sadly warped outlook of the writer over the decade from 1822 to 1832 emerges from them.

The rectory was immediately adjacent to the Manor House owned by Mrs Jarret, of whom Skinner was pathologically suspicious. She wished to persuade him to move elsewhere and pass the living to her son-in-law, named

*The church in the Somerset valley below Camerton, close to Bath, where the Rev. John Skinner held the living in the early part of the nineteenth century, still an area with an aura of its own.*

Gooch, on suitable terms, but he would not accept her proposals. He recorded in July 1822:

'Thursday, July 25th. . . . I . . . reverted to my first declaration, that it would not suit me to take less than the sum I had specified (£450) that the proposition of my letting my glebe and giving up the Parsonage to Mr Gooch had originated in her, that I never should have thought of leaving my charge if they had not, of late especially, conducted themselves in such a manner as to shew they purposely kicked against all authority; but if I continued amongst them I should exert the powers I possessed, and although an unpleasant contest might ensue, I was prepared to go through with it, and doubted not that in the end I should be successful. . . . As I perceived a carriage driving up to the door I took my leave. . . . The plain state of the case is, if Mrs Jarret, by making my situation uncomfortable, could drive me from it, get the Living on her own terms, and open the way for Mr Gooch to step into my Parsonage, her policy would succeed; but I am not to be frightened by the opposition of the lower orders, even headed by herself . . .'

He found the Methodists a constant trial and wrote:

'Thursday, September 5. I called on the invalids immediately after breakfast and found Cottle's daughter very much worse. Adam Nash's wife was with her, a thoroughbred Methodist. How strange it is these people will interfere and thwart and pervert all the efforts of the regular clergy. Indeed our advice is held of little value. Adam Nash, the collier, himself pretends to know far more than I know. . . . I have often thought that some of the more steady and serious among the Methodists might be of great service to the regular clergy, if they would keep within certain bounds. . . . As they know far better the private life and disposition of the poorer orders they might give some very useful information to the clergyman when he went to visit the sick. In the Primitive Church there were evidently persons of this description by the name of Catechumens, who were of great assistance to the parochial minister. But alas! the present Methodists set up their opinions in opposition to those of the clergyman, they in fact endeavour to convert him; and look upon him as little better than a castaway if he cannot feel as they feel. . . . A clergyman nowadays has indeed a difficult task to perform.'

In March 1823 his tactlessness no doubt exacerbated ill-feeling between himself and the Manor House. He noted:

'Sunday, March 16. Very few people at Church. Not seeing Mrs Jarrot and her daughter there, I called at the Manor House to enquire respecting them and was shewn into the drawing-room, where I saw Mr and Mrs Gooch writing letters: the former apologised for not having attended to the duty of the day. I told him no apology was necessary to me, since his own conscience must tell him what was best to be done in such matters . . .'

Later that day Mrs Gooch tried to get her revenge, but Skinner missed the point and recorded:

'As soon as the service was concluded I called at the Manor House to enquire after Mrs Gooch, who had quitted the Church at the beginning of the Litany, and, as her husband followed her, I was apprehensive of her being ill, but learnt there was nothing of. consequence the matter. Surely the Church is too solemn a place to trifle with, as with a drawing room and a clergyman above all ought to have some paramount reason for quitting it . . .'

In August he tried to persuade Mrs Jarret to subscribe towards building a new school, without much success, and wrote:

'Sunday, August 10. I preached on the morning at Camerton a sermon pointing out the advantages of education if properly directed and the ills arising from the neglect of it. Mrs Jarret, I thought, did not seem to approve of some parts of the discourse, as I now and then noticed an emphatic "hem." However I am too old a soldier to be alarmed at squibs!'

Although his brother Russell undertook the tedious job of deciphering his writing and making fair copies of his Journals it was typical of Skinner that he could note:

'Monday, October 6. I was busily occupied this morning in correcting some of the Journals, which I am sorry to see have been transcribed in to too great a hurry by brother . . .'

Two days later, called to a parishioner's deathbed he wrote:

'Wednesday, October 8. . . . On arriving at Gullick's we found the family in a sad state, the poor woman being just dead, the children, seven in number, crying round their father . . .

'Thursday, October 9. . . . I . . . called at Gullick's where the family were all at dinner. The sorrow of the children is vehement at first, but soon wears off; the poor man will feel it much more, because he will find his own comfort so much connected with his loss. But happy is it that people in the lower ranks of life are not possessed of the same sensibility as their superiors; certain am I that all things are conducted on a much more equal footing than they appear to be at first sight — if enjoyment be less, privation is in proportion.'

His description of employing a servant shortly afterwards is indicative of his methods of making himself popular:

'Tuesday, October 21. I walked to the Glebe House after breakfast and spoke to John Cook on the subject of his going there. I told him candidly that I had met with so much dishonesty and deception from the Camerton people, I was almost determined never to employ one of them again in my service; however, I would give him a trial to Lady Day. I then hinted at his wife being too fond of dress, saying that young Widcombe would have been now in prosperity had it not been for the misconduct of his wife in the first instance, which influenced his own. The man listened attentively and replied I should never have reason to accuse him of dishonesty, and he should endeavour to do everything to show his gratitude. I agreed to pay him eight shillings a week till

Lady Day, as the house is worth fully two shillings a week more, indeed, he paid as much for the one he now occupied. I moreover gave him a crop of potatoes in the garden, which is fully worth five pounds, so that he begins his career under easy circumstances as far as respects myself, and I only hope he has no old debts to liquidate . . .'

Other examples of how he unconsciously made himself unpopular were recorded in November and December:

'Sunday, November 30. [After conducting a service for a neighbouring clergyman he visited the dying landlord of the Red Post Public House] . . . I found Mr West smoking and drinking there; on my telling him it was contrary to the regulations of the magistrates to be in a public house during the time of Church Service, he was disposed to kick against their authority, but became more submissive when I spoke firmly to him.

'Thursday, December 4. I received a bill of £8. 5s. 0d. from Cruttwell the lawyer, absolutely for doing nothing. This is the second time I have paid him the same amount for merely writing letters to the tithepayers without taking any further trouble. I shall certainly freely express my sentiments.'

At Christmas he had a bad cold, which may excuse his comments:

'Thursday, December 25. I cannot say my sleep was disturbed, but my waking hours certainly were by the ringing of the bells about seven o'clock announcing the joyous day, when half the Parish at least will be drunk. Mr Hammond performed evening service. . . . I was occupied part of the morning in reading the Hebrew Bible.'

Two days later he recorded one aftermath:

'Saturday, December 27. Smallcombe, who was married on Christmas Day and whose wife was brought to bed the same day, sent his child to be named, as they are fearful it will die.'

In 1826 there was a major domestic upset. He noted:

'Wednesday, February 1. . . . my mind is quite unhinged; indeed, the misconduct of my housekeeper, Mrs Williams, continues to add to the irritation of my nerves. She was so excessivegly insolent because Hester is permitted to return to work in the garden that I was obliged to dismiss her, and give her a month's wages in order to be rid of her. The servants had one and all complained of her abusive language, but she had been careful not to employ it against myself till this evening, when she used the coarsest expressions, and even oaths, so that there was no choice left me. I gave her a draft on my banker before I went to bed, and took her receipt for the same, to which Betty was witness, and desired her to leave the premises early the next day, before I went to Bath. I am convinced my servants are in part influenced by the malignant neighborhood against their master, and induced to forget the respect they ought to show him. These are indeed evils. I could bear all outside my roof, that is, in the Parish and in the world, when my books are my companions and my friends within doors; but if I am unsettled and distorted in my own family and at my own fireside, it is indeed then a trial.'

Altogether 1826 was a bad year, for Owen who had been sent to Oxford was in trouble, and Joseph who was at Sandhurst was all but expelled. In January 1727 matters came to a head and he recorded:

'Monday, January 1. 1827. I read the official letter from Sandhurst respecting Joseph, which was by no means what I had wished, and worried me much. I spoke to him after dinner on the subject, and I am sorry to say, with less coolness than I ought to have done; reproof loses much of its effect when delivered hastily, but I fear no reproof will be of much service. I found myself so unwell and so much affected, I went to bed before nine o'clock.

'Tuesday, January 2. . . . I find my sons and daughter have cost me this year nearly £500, and as much last year, which is more than my housekeeping and establishment amounts to. I have spent nothing extra on myself, if I except my journey to Town, which cost me £30 and was partly on business . . .

'Wednesday, January 3. . . . About the middle of the day my sons set off in the car for Southfield, and I on foot, as I preferred walking. . . . My son overtook me in the car just beyond Babington, and on my asking them why they had been so tardy . . . I am sorry to say replied in a manner very unbecoming them to utter, or myself to hear. It was indeed a severe pang, but I have experienced so many of late it did not entirely overcome me. . . . To be kicked and buffeted by my own offspring is indeed a trial, but God's will be done . . .

'Friday, January 5. I went to bed before eleven, but not to sleep. I am sorely wounded in the tenderest point — my mind. It is a bad beginning to the New Year . . .'

This was the first of the family rows which were from this point on to become a feature of his household, averaging about one major confrontation a year. In this case Joseph was withdrawn from Sandhurst and took charge of the glebe farm, while Owen returned to Oxford. Meanwhile Skinner continued to discharge his parish·duties as conscientiously as before, although continually complaining of the conduct of everyone concerned, as for instance early in 1828:

'Saturday, January 19. . . . My worthy parishioners begin to amuse themselves again; twice this week they have tied a tin pot to the tail of my dog, merely to annoy and exasperate me. However, I must think as little as possible about them, since I have things of more consequence to attend to . . .'

Lacking humour, he was a constant prey to real or imagined insults:

'Saturday, February 9. . . . I drove to Mells to attend a clerical meeting. . . . We sat down fourteen to dinner, which was an uncomfortable one owing to there only being one waiter. After some rather desultory conversation one of the party, by the name of Bumstead, asked me what was the etymon of his name. I did not perceive it at the time, but have every reason to believe, on account of what afterwards occurred, that it was done purposely to put me on the subject of Etymology for the amusement of the company. . . . It was nearly ten o'clock when I arrived at my quiet parsonage. . . . I went to bed a little after ten, not altogether pleased with myself or my associates. If it were not for the sake of my family I would now follow the bent of my own inclinations and devote the rest of my life to a proper regulation of my thoughts, words and actions, which can best be done in solitude, when I enter into society I can do neither . . . Anna is engaged in teaching the servants write and cypher, from nine o'clock till they come to prayers. I hope it will be of service, but I begin to have doubts about teaching the lower orders beyond reading . . .'

The state of tension under which he lived is revealed in one entry:

'Sunday, April 21. I slept but little last night; my nerves are in a constant state of irritability, which I endeavour to counteract by every means in my power . . .'

By the end of July the domestic storm which had been brewing finally broke and he sent Anna and Joseph to stay with his mother, to whom he had already despatched Owen. He wrote to her:

'July 28. My dear Mother,

It is with the most heartfelt regret that I again request your assistance in receiving Anna and Joseph. . . . I will not worry you or myself with particulars; thank God I am now calm and shall continue so when the cause which has made me otherwise is removed. . . . My own mind tells me I have done everything I ought to do for my *ungrateful children*. . . . You may be perfectly easy on my account, as I know as soon as I resume my studies and am freed from the constant irritation I have been exposed to in my own house, I shall be *myself again*. Yours very truly John Skinner. P.S The origin

of all the evil I complain of in my sons is *Idleness* and a want
of proper principles . . .'

Not unnaturally this created something of a sensation
locally as Skinner himself soon learned:

'Friday, August 1. . . . Hammond told me that a gentleman in Bath said to him the other day: "So there are strange
doings at Camerton Parsonage; Mr Skinner has turned his
children out of doors," or words to that effect and that he
replied that he knew that was not the case since they were
then on a visit to their Grandmother.

'My wound is so painful of itself that I shall not heed this
additional smart; besides, after all, it is only self-love which is
wounded by the opinions of others . . .'

Yet he could also record:

'Sunday, August 31. . . . As I walked back home from
Church I saw my poor old horse so lame he could not put
one of his feet to the ground. I accordingly sent . . . to the
farrier, who came before dark and said it was merely a corn.
I hope it may prove to be as he says, for the old horse is such
a favourite I cannot bear to have him suffer any unnecessary
pain . . .'

By September his sons and daughter were once again
reconciled and at home, at least temporarily. Owen, unable
to make headway at Oxford went instead to Cambridge.
Joseph continued in charge of the glebe farm, living at
Camerton with Anna. For the rest of 1828 and throughout
1829 there were no further major incidents, only minor
family quarrels, although his relationship with his
parishioners remained strained. Early in 1830 he wrote:

'Sunday, January 10. I felt uncomfortably irritated by the
behaviour of the people . . . if the patient Job had been
Rector of Camerton he might not have been such a celebrity
on account of that virtue.

'I know my infirmity, which is too great irritability, yet I
endeavour to correct it; of one thing I am certain, I never
retain the unwelcome guest beyond the impulse of the

moment, and every hour of my existence at this place is so exposed to insult that one must be a stick or a stone not to feel it . . .'

He was always quick to imagine insults and slights:

'Saturday, January 16. . . . Sir Richard Hoare never used to omit sending me some game at Christmas. I fear . . . he is . . . hurt because I differ from him . . . and am about to publish what I have written on the subject of Camelodunum. I have observed a difference in his manner towards me, but this may only be imagination; time will shew. Thank God I never solicit nor care for the worldly countenance of any man; I am too proud to solicit patronage.'

Under his son Joseph's careful management he recorded a successful tithe-paying, but even then noted one source of irritation:

'Monday, April 5th. It was a beautiful morning. I went to receive my composition for tithe of the farmers, this being the day appointed for their payment. Joseph had previously written out the memoranda of the payment of each individual so that there was no difficulty or delay. There were sixteen sat down to dinner and everything went off very well, as all the farmers were very civil, excepting John Rossiter, who has taken Keel's farm. Ever since I dismissed him from the office of churchwarden . . . he has carefully avoided touching his hat to me . . . which is certainly of no consequence whatever to me; but when he has the meanness to eat at my expense and behave in that manner it is going rather too far . . .'

Seizing the moment when he was in a good mood Joseph appears to have tried to explain some home truths to him as he noted:

'Joseph . . . as we rode homewards, told me that I had taken a pack of fancies into my head without any foundation; although people did say queer things of me it was true, and not without reason. When I asked him to explain what he meant and that it was the duty of a son to acquaint his Father of whatever was said to his disadvantage, in order to give him an opportunity of meeting his adversaries, he then said I had no adversaries but in my own imagination; that I treated my children like servants and not sons; that Mrs Jarrett he thought a very civil, good sort of woman, and that I was to blame for not behaving in a more neighbourly manner to her. As I found that this kind of conversation only contributed to excite the irritation I wished to get rid of, I rode on, leaving Joseph behind!'

In July, he learned of the quite unexpected death of Mrs Jarrett, his neighbour. He wrote of her funeral:

'Tuesday, July 27. . . . I went to the Manor House at two o'clock. . . . About three Mr Gooch and Mr Stephen Jarrett coming into the parlour, I shook hands very cordially . . . and I really felt for them as though they had been my relations. How trifling are all our little heartburnings and differences when we see the cause which excited them humbled in the dust and are well assured we shall shortly ourselves be tenants of the grave. I felt much during the service, but was able to read it with composure . . .'

Without Mrs Jarrett as a focal point and safety valve for his feelings, inevitably he soon had another major row with his family. He described it at length:

'Monday, September 20. After dinner some conversation took place about a trifle, between my daughter and myself; her brother Owen took her part and it ended in just such a scene as has been before acted; everything that could be said or done to irritate me my son employed and unfortunately succeeded. . . . I said . . . that when he left my roof I should feel relieved. . . . He said he . . . should be glad to be quit of my house and never see my face again. He and his sister chose to go to bed before Prayers. I read to the servants and with a heavy heart retired to bed but not to rest.

'No-one excepting my brother who transcribes this will read the sad recital. When I am dead and fifty years have passed over my grave, and when this base and ungrateful son has finished his career, someone who peruses my Journals will read this as they would a novel and think the recital has been heightened through feelings wounded almost to the pitch of madness, but this is not the case . . .'

For several pages he rambled on at length giving the lie to his own statements and indicating very clearly how upset he was. His entries for the next two days indicate his reactions:

'Tuesday, September 21. I left Owen and his sister to Breakfast in the parlour and had some tea sent up into my study; I could not eat anything the whole day and went to bed early.

'Wednesday, September 22. When I was in the greatest distress imaginable yesterday, Owen was amusing himself with his lathe and my daughter with her usual occupations. I attribute a great deal of the misery I experience to sending my Sons to Winchester College, where they were educated. During the time of their abode there the boys were two or three times in a state of rebellion against their masters and brought the same feelings home with them against their parent . . .'

Extraordinarily enough after four days this tremendous domestic storm in a teacup was at least temporarily calmed and he recorded:

'Thursday, September 23. My daughter came before dinner and said she was very sorry for the uneasiness she had given me, and hoped I would pass it over; and that with respect to Owen, as the dispute began with her she hoped I would not think of it any more . . .

'I said I knew my infirmity, and all that I could do was to keep out of the way of those who would purposely provoke me; and was it not their duty to put up with a few angry words spoken in the heat of the moment. . . . If Owen had anything to say . . . I was ready to listen . . . and forgive him as I had done her . . .'

After a lengthy session of an hour father and son were

again reconciled and ultimately Joseph also. The family concord lasted uneasily until the following October of 1831 when another fearful row developed with Owen openly calling his father a madman and all being duly recorded. There was then yet another reconciliation and in 1832 Joseph fell ill with consumption, the disease which had already killed so many of the family. It was soon clear that he was dying, but even this did not prevent the family wrangles from continuing, if in a somewhat muted form. Then in October 1832 cholera broke out locally and Skinner, faced with a real crisis, rose to the occasion:

'Saturday, October 13. After breakfast I received a letter from Mr Lawton the bailiff at the coal works, announcing the breaking out of cholera at Camerton. I immediately walked to his house, taking with me some camphor and aromatic vinegar to give him. This being pay day with the colliers it occurred to me that if the infection be among them he must take every precaution to avoid it. . . . I immediately wrote to Curtis the apothecary, desiring him to come to Camerton. I also saw Cook, the father of the boy who died and now lies in the same house with his grandmother, and said he must get the bodies put instantly in coffins and interred out of the way. I then spoke to White about digging a deep grave in the churchyard out of the line where the bodies are now interred . . .

'Curtis, accompanied by Flower, the apothecary from Chilcompton, came to me . . . and said that prompt measures must be taken to prevent the spreading of the infection. . . . They said it was much better that I did not officiate at the funeral; that at other places it was not done. I said I should be guided by the feelings of the people themselves who attended the funeral, for if I shewed myself fearful of catching the complaint while interring the body, it would have the effect of deterring them from bringing it to the grave and of assisting at all at the interment.

'I ordered the man at the shop to distribute two ounces of

camphor among the people, who came to his house and desired him to say to them, if they kept a little in the mouth now and then it would be beneficial as a preventive.

'I also told the clerk to purchase on my account at the public-house a bottle of spirits to give a glass to each of the people who attended the funeral. . . . I determined to read the Funeral Service, which I did . . . after dinner and saw the grave filled in . . .

'I desired the schoolmistress to dismiss the girls' school till the disorder was abated . . .'

On the Sunday he visited the sick and, learning of three further deaths, ordered more graves to be dug and arrangements made. He wrote:

'Monday, October 15. . . . I walked into the village to enquire after the sick and see if I could be of any service . . . I spoke afterwards to Green, the under-bailiff of the coal works, and told him he should see that the drains were opened and the dung heaps removed or put into a hole in their gardens. He said, *it was the Lord's will they should die and he could not prevent it.* I said he was a greater fool than I had supposed him to be, and if he would not see it done I would speak to Lawton, the overlooker of the collieries, who would enforce the performance of what the laws enjoined. This seemed to have its weight and he said he would see that the nuisances were removed . . .'

He was asked to stay with friends nearby but wrote that he 'would be a poltroon to desert my post when the enemy was about to attack it.' However he also noted: 'I shall get Anna to return to Bath tomorrow to be with her brother [Joseph], and then I shall be at liberty to perform my duty without distressing her feelings.'

An emergency of this nature suited his psychopathic personality admirably. It kept him busy making decisions and his hectoring manner was just what was required to stir people from their apathy. He continued to visit the sick until November, when the worst was over. By this time his son

Joseph was very near his end and had returned to Camerton with his brother and sister.

With the end of the emergency, although his son was dying, Skinner reverted to his old form and quarrelled with his family. The old tensions revived, even on the subject of giving religious consolation to the dying Joseph. Then in mid-November 1832 the diary suddenly ended at the stage reached by Skinner's brother Russell before his death in December. Not long afterwards his son Joseph also died. Without even the consolation of his Journals it is not surprising that seven years later Skinner felt he could go on no longer. The one hundred and fifty volumes of his Journals were bequeathed to the British Museum. The private torment they disclosed was finally ended one misty evening by a shotgun blast in the wood behind Camerton rectory. Thus, finally, John Skinner achieved the peace he had sought for so vainly throughout his life at Camerton.

# 12

## The Rev. Francis Kilvert

### Victorian Curate: Welsh Borders

*We played croquet and lawn tennis in a drizzling rain*

Francis Kilvert was born at Hardenhuish near Chippenham in Wiltshire in 1840, son of the Rev. Robert Kilvert, vicar of that parish, who also ran a small school to eke out his income and so educated his two sons and three daughters privately. Francis Kilvert went on to Wadham College, Oxford and took Holy Orders. His father meanwhile had accepted the living of Langley Burrell, also in Wiltshire, his wife being related to the Squire, with whom he had an uneasy relationship. Here Francis Kilvert served his first curacy before going in 1865 to act as curate under the Rev. Richard Venables, vicar of Clyro in Radnorshire. In 1872 he returned to Langley Burrell. In 1876 he accepted the living of St. Harmon's in Radnorshire, but at this point there is a gap in his diaries, which start again in 1877, when he accepted the living of Bredwardine in Herefordshire. There he spent little more than eighteen months before his early death in 1879 at the age of thirty-nine, some five weeks after his marriage.

From 1865 to 1879 Francis Kilvert kept a series of diaries, of which twenty-two have survived and have been edited in three volumes by William Plomer, the first edition of which was published in 1938. They provide an interesting picture

*The church at Langley Burrell, close to Chippenham, in Wiltshire, where the Rev. Francis Kilvert spent his youth and where he was curate from 1863-4 and from 1872-6.*

of a Victorian country curate's life in the Welsh Borders as well as a rounded portrait of the man himself. He was a great walker, though possibly never really robust. Interested in people, poor or rich, young or old, he was of a gentle, poetic and happy nature. Frequently lovelorn, he was on several occasions gently requested by parents to withdraw his attentions from their daughters.

Unlike Jones, who was married and rearing a large family as a curate, Kilvert really did not have enough to do. Surrounded largely by females in his work, his attitudes and interests probably grew unconsciously rather feminine as a result. Like Charles Dodgson, better known as Lewis Carroll, he took an innocent delight in young girls. He was clearly a very late developer in many ways and, basically, a happy, poetic, dreamer.

It is not perhaps surprising that Woodforde and Kilvert, the lengthiest clerical diarists produced in volume form, have become almost cult figures, with societies named after them. Of the two there is no doubt that Kilvert was by far the better descriptive writer on the country scene. It was perhaps as well, however, that he died when he did, for had he lived on to become a hen-pecked husband like William Jones, or if some of his more unfortunate fantasies had developed into vices in old age, it would have been truly regrettable.

In 1878 he was offered the Chaplaincy of Cannes and it is possible that had he taken it he might have lived longer and provided further interesting French chapters in his diary. Yet, though he was incumbent of both St. Harmon's and Bredwardine there is comparatively little about them included in the diaries, compared with what goes before. It is principally as a curate therefore that he must be remembered. From his diaries there emerges the perfect portrait of a Victorian curate in the Welsh Border country, lovelorn, poetic, longing passionately for the unattainable, attending amiably to his duties throughout the parish and liked by all.

It was not all vicarage tea parties by any means, as he made clear when describing the fierce winter weather at Clyro in February 1870:

'Septuagesima Sunday, St. Valentine's Eve, (13th February). Preached at Clyro in the morning. . . . Very few people in the Church, the weather fearful, violent deadly E. wind and the hardest frost we have had yet. Went to Bettws in the afternoon wrapped in two waistcoats, two coats, a muffler and a mackintosh and was not at all too warm. . . . When I got to the Chapel my beard, moustaches and whiskers were so stiff with ice that I could hardly open my mouth and my beard was frozen onto my mackintosh. There was a large christening party from Llwyn Gwilym. . . . The baby was baptised in ice which was broken and swimming about in the Font. A sad day for mother and child to come out. Dined at the Vicarage.'

Unlike the Rev. John Skinner, he could talk to his parishioners and share their feelings. Two consecutive entries in April reveal this and something of his relationship with his vicar, the Rev. Richard Venables:

'Friday, 8 April. In the green lane . . . I came upon Smith of Wernwg hedging. He told me that a child had arrived at Pen-y-wyrlod and wanted to know if something cannot be done to separate Stephen Davies and Myra Rees. I said there was no law to prevent people living in concubinage. People are very indignant about this affair and think it is a great scandal to the parish, and rightly so. But what is to be done? The man's family are mad with him especially Mrs Smith of New Barn, but no one has any influence over him. He is infatuated with the girl, whose tongue is so desperate and unscrupulous that everyone is afraid of her . . .

'Saturday, 9 April. . . . Consulted Mr V. about Stephen Davies and Myra Rees but he does not see what can be done . . .'

His entry for Easter was in his best lyrical style on the subject of grave dressing:

'Easter Day, 17 April. The happiest, brightest, and most beautiful Easter I have ever spent. I woke early and looked out. As I had hoped the day was cloudless, a glorious morning. . . . I got up between five and six and was out soon after six. . . . Last night poor Mrs Chalmers was in trouble because she had not been able to get any flowers to dress her husband's grave and Miss Chalmers was in deep distress about it. . . . So I thought I would go and gather some primroses and flower the grave for them. . . . I got a good handful with plenty of green leaves and brought them home. . . . I made a simple cross upon it [the grave] with my five primrose bunches. . . . I went to the house . . . and got the primroses which had been in water all night and . . . with these five bunches I made a primrose cross on the turf at the foot of the white marble cross which marks Mr Henry Venables' grave. . . . People came to look at the crosses and they were much admired. Then I ran home to dress and snatch a mouthful of breakfast. . . . After morning service I took Mr V. round the churchyard and showed him the crosses on his mother's, wife's and brother's graves. He was quite taken by surprise and very much gratified. I am glad to see that our primrose crosses seem to be having some effect for I think I notice this Easter some attempt to copy them and an advance towards the form of the cross in some of the decorations of the graves. I wish we could get the people to adopt some little design in the disposition of the flowers upon the graves instead of sticking sprigs into the turf aimlessly anywhere, anyhow and with no meaning at all. But one does not like to interfere too much with their artless, natural way of showing their respect and love for the dead. I am thankful to find this beautiful custom on the increase . . .'

He was a considerable walker, but even so, according to his diary, he was prepared to go to enormous lengths for very simple pleasures:

'Tuesday, 3 May. Started at noon to walk to Newchurch. . . . By Tyn-y-cwm Meadows to Newchurch village and on turning in at the old Vicarage garden door I heard the hum of the little school. . . . The curate and his eldest daughter were away and pretty Emmeline in a russet brown stuff dress and her long fair curls was keeping school bravely with an austere look on her severe beautiful face, and hearing little Polly Greenway read. Janet and Matilda dressed just alike in black silk skirts, scarlet bodices and white pinafores, and with blue ribbons in their glossy, bonny dark brown curls were sitting on a form at a long desk with the other children working at sums. Janet was doing simple division and said she had done five sums, whereupon I kissed her and she was nothing loth. Moreover I offered to give her a kiss for every sum, at which she laughed. As I stood by the window making notes . . . Janet kept on interrupting her work to glance round at me shyly but saucily with her mischievous beautiful grey eyes. Shall I confess that I travelled ten miles today over the hills for a kiss, to kiss that child's sweet face. Ten miles for a kiss . . .'

He took care to try and spread good feeling throughout his parish in simple effective ways as an entry later in May makes clear:

'Thursday, 12 May. Painscastle Fair, one of the two they have there in the year and Mr Wilson of the Dyffryn (the farmer from whose stable Margaret Griffith's son stole the mare this spring) overtook me riding a chestnut pony to the fair. I asked him to call on Margaret Griffiths and speak kindly to her and comfort her about it next time he goes through the village, and he said he would call on rent day, tomorrow week. I think this will be a help and comfort to her for she has been abashed and distressed ever since, thinking people were looking coldly on her . . .'

He recorded occasional simple instances of village life in perfect vignettes, as for instance:

'Wednesday, 8 June. As I was writing a sermon . . . a note was brought me from David Vaughan and his son William was waiting outside. So I had him in and gave him some beer. He was rather shy and constrained and sat for a long time quite still with the tumbler of beer in his hand and looking at nothing. I could not conceive why he did not drink the beer. Then I thought he was ill. At last he faced round on his chair half wheel, and pronounced solemnly and formally "My best respects to you, Sir." After having delivered himself of this respectful sentiment he imbibed some beer. It was a bit of perfect good breeding. . . .'

Many pages of his diary contained revealing passages of prose with suppressed undertones of passion:

'Saturday, 9 July. It is a pretty lane this Bird's Nest Lane, very shady and quiet, narrow and overbowered here and there with arching wyches and hazels. Sometimes my darling child Gipsy comes down to school this way . . . often and often must those tiny feet have trodden this stony narrow green-arched lane and those sweet blue eyes have looked down this vista to the blue mountains and those little hands have gathered flowers along these banks. O my child if you did but know . . . that this lane and this dingle and these fields are sweet to me and holy ground for your sweet sake. . . . Ah Gipsy . . .'

Even the view from his bedroom window to the 'white farm house of Penllan' on the hill could give rise to thoughts of the pretty young milkmaid there:

'Monday, 11 July. . . . before the sun has touched the sleeping village . . . he has stolen into her bedroom and crept along the wall from chair to chair till he has reached the bed, and has kissed the fair hand and arm that lies upon the coverlet and the white bosom that heaves half uncovered after the restlessness of the sultry night, and has kissed her mouth whose scarlet lips just parting in a smile and pouting like rosebuds to be kissed, show the pearly gleam of the white teeth, and has kissed the sweet face and the blue veined silky lashed eyelids and the white brow and the soft bright tangled hair till she has unclosed the sweetest eyes that ever open to the dawn . . .'

Probably due to his upbringing in the vicarage at Harden-huish he obtained a real delight in both giving and receiving gifts. A good instance of this was shown by an entry in October:

'Monday, 24 October. Last night, when I went into the Vicarage to dinner, just as I entered the drawing room, a small strange clock struck seven. Mr V. said it was a clock he was taking charge of for Mrs H. Venables. After dinner he showed it to me. It was a beautiful little travelling clock in its leather case, brass and glass, showing the works, and striking the hours and half hours on a sweet soft bell. "There is an inscription on it," he said, "if you can read it." On the foot of the clock I saw inscribed as I held it up the candle, "R.F. Kilvert from J.C. Venables." How kind. What a beautiful and unexpected present. How little when I heard the small strange clock strike and asked whose it was, that it was mine. The clock is from Nathan's at Birmingham, chosen by Mr Knightly Howman, and I fear must have been very expensive. I carried my treasure home, took it up to my bedroom and heard the sweet low soft bell striking in the night . . .'

He was fond of animals and often mentioned his favourite cat, Toby, as in a typical daily entry in November:

'Monday, 28 November. A plaintive mew outside the door. I open the door and tabby Toby comes trotting in with his funny little note of affection.

'When visiting John Morgan of the New Inn I asked him if he trusted that he was forgiven by God. "I cannot answer you fully," he said. "I make my appeals to Him," said the sick man solemnly.

'Baskerville sent me a brace of pheasants. I put up a notice of the next Penny Reading in the Post Office window and called at Annie Powell's and found her better. Walked up the Cwm and found old James Jones stonebreaking. He told me how he was once travelling from Hereford to Hay by coach when the coach was wrecked in a flood by Bredwardine Bridge because the coachman would not take the bearing reins off the horse . . .'

On occasions without any clear explanation he would give vent to his feelings in a very definite manner:

'Saturday, 17 December. That liar and thief of the world Sarah Thomas, Mrs Chaloner's servant is gone. The evening she went no one knew what had become of her all the early part of the night. Probably she passed it under some hedge and not alone. At a quarter before midnight she asked for a bed which Mrs Price very properly refused. I hope she has cleared out of this village. Beast.'

His daily life could be spartan enough in wintertime as he noted:

'Sunday, Christmas Day. As I lay awake praying in the early morning I thought I heard a sound of distant bells. It was an intense frost. I sat down in my bath upon a sheet of thick ice which broke in the middle into large pieces whilst sharp points and jagged edges stuck all round the sides of the tub . . . not particularly comforting to the naked thighs and loins, for the keen ice cut like broken glass. The ice water stung and scorched like fire. I had to collect the floating pieces of ice and pile them on a chair before I could use the sponge and then I had to thaw the sponge in my hands for it was a mass of ice. . . . Walked to the Sunday School with Gibbins and the road sparkled with millions of rainbows, the seven colours gleaming in every glittering point of hoar frost. The Church was very cold in spite of two roaring stove fires. Mr V. preached and went to Bettws.'

During a visit to London in January 1871 he innocently entered a photograph shop in the Burlington Arcade, then notorious for the salacity of many of the shops as well as for its streetwalkers. His reception casts a revealing sidelight on Victorian morality:

'Thursday, 12 January. . . . In the Arcade I went into a photograph shop . . . and asked if he had a photograph of the picture "Rock of Ages". . . . A dark French-looking bearded man was reading a paper behind the counter. He got up and looked at me steadily and then backed away towards the fire to get away as far as possible. "No Sir," he said sternly after scrutinising me narrowly. . . . His manner was very curious and he was evidently very uneasy and anxious to get me out of the shop as quickly as possible. . . . Opposite the Charing Cross Hotel I met Sam and . . . he explained the mystery. . . . The man is notorious for selling obscene French photographs. . . . He thought I was a spy . . .'

Although unsophisticated in London, Kilvert was accustomed to the ways of the countryside, but even he found the strange practices of some of his more backward parishioners in Clyro almost unbelievable:

'Wednesday, February . . . 1. Sarah Witney . . . told me that Mrs Jones, the jockey's wife at the corner had a fortnight ago left some linen drying out on the churchyard hedge all night having forgotten to take it in. By morning Mrs Jones declared two pairs of drawers and a "shimmy" had been stolen and her suspicions fell on some of the neighbours. She and her husband consulted the ordeal of the key and the Bible (turning the key in the Bible) The Key said, "Bella Whitney." Then Jones the jockey went to the brickyard and got some clay which he made into a ball. Inside the ball he put a live toad. The clay ball was either boiled or put into the fire and during the process of boiling or baking the toad was expected to scratch the name of the thief upon a piece of paper put into the clay ball along with him. Some other horrible charm was used to discover the thief, the figure of a person being pricked out on a piece of clay. It is almost incredible.'

He was not a fast reader to judge by his entries, for he started reading *Puck* by Ouida in October 1870, noting that 'the authoress seems to have a rabid hatred of women and parsons' and it was not until February 1871 that he recorded this somewhat muddled criticism:

'Tuesday, 7 February. Finished reading *Puck*, clever, bitter, extravagant, full of repetitions and absurdities and ludicrous ambitious attempts at fine writing, weak and bombastic. The great blot is the insane and vicious hatred of women. Evidently written by a woman.'

Like most curates he seems to have had little head for drink as he indicated with his usual profusion of adjectives when describing the effects of drinking too much port:

'Wednesday, March 1. After dinner last night Mr V. kindly anxious to cure my face ache made me drink four large glasses of port. The consequence was that all night and all today I have been groaning with a bursting raging splitting sick headache.'

Similar to many Victorians, Kilvert was a very late developer. During his mid-thirties he was in an almost continual state of passion for some female or another. In September 1871 the object of his ardour was Daisy (or Fanny) Thomas, aged nineteen, youngest daughter of a Major Thomas one of his parishioners. He recorded anguished entries on the subject daily. He met her when playing croquet and wrote:

'Friday, 9 September. Perhaps this may be a memorable day in my life. . . . Today I fell in love with Fanny Thomas. . . . It was a very happy evening. How little I knew what was in store for me when I came to Llan Thomas this afternoon . . .

'Sunday 10. . . . I have been in a fever all day about Daisy . . .

'Monday 11. . . . Still I was very restless and feverish . . .

'Tuesday 12. . . . A wretched restless feverish night . . .

'Wednesday 13. . . . An ever memorable day in my life. . . . I started off for Llan Thomas on foot rather nervous . . . we went out into the garden her father and I . . . "I-am-attached-to-one-of-your-daughters," I said . . . he seemed a good deal taken aback. . . . He said . . . he could not allow an engagement under the circumstances. . . . I went back . . . with a sorrowful heart.

'Thursday, 14. . . . Somehow things seem to look brighter and more cheerful this morning . . .

'Friday 15. . . . Lying in bed this morning dozing . . . I composed my speech of thanks at my wedding breakfast . . .

'Monday 18. . . . I love her more and more each time I see her . . .

'Wednesday 20. . . . it seemed to me as if she had received a hint not to be too forthcoming . . .

'Saturday 23. A letter came from Mr Thomas. Kindly expressed and cordial, but bidding me to give up all thoughts and hopes of Daisy. . . . I felt very sad. The sun seemed to have gone out of the sky. . . . I wrote a courteous reply saying that I must abide by his decision . . . all that was left me was hope . . .'

As late as November he was still 'hoping', but after that the romance slowly faded away, and, sad to relate, poor Daisy Thomas ended her days a spinster.

Whatever else he may have been, poet, observer, cleric, lover, Kilvert was no sportsman and never set out to be one. His views in the matter were set out in an entry in November:

'Monday, 13 November. "What a fine day it is. Let us go out and kill something." The old reproach against the English.

'The Squire has just gone by with a shooting party. A line of gentlemen walking first followed by the keepers carrying guns and . . . beaters and boys and dogs and hangers on . . .'

By the following year he had made up his mind to leave Clyro and entered in his diary:

'Tuesday, 26 March. . . . To-day I wrote to the Bishop of St. David's to give notice that I intend to resign the Curacy of Clyro on the 1st of July next, "when (I added by Mr Venable's advice, but against my own wish) I shall have been a licensed curate in the same parish in your Lordship's diocese for seven years and a half" . . . '

His parish visiting was a duty which he seemd to enjoy and carried out conscientiously:

'Saturday, 13 April. . . . I went to see old Price who is in a miserable state. . . . That miser, curmudgeon and villain and beast, Watkins of Cross-Foot, his son-in-law, has left him to his fate and will not let his wife come near her father or help him in any way. The Lord reward him according to his works.

'The poor old man was lying alone this afternoon parched with thirst. "I'm very droughty," he murmured feebly. I went home and got him some brandy and water and gave it him. His gratitude for this little attention was very touching. "I hope," said the old man solemnly, "you will be remembered in heaven."

'The two old women Hannah Jones and Sarah Probert were both lying in bed and groaning horribly. I gave them some money and their cries and groans suddenly ceased . . .'

His natural good manners led Kilvert to do much that he would have preferred to avoid. A good instance was recorded in April:

'Saturday, April 20. . . . As I was taking my ticket, Hughes, Rector of Bryngwyn, clapped me on the back. He was going to Hay, so out of politeness I was obliged to go third class with him though I had paid for a second class ticket. I had much rather have gone alone for I hate talking while travelling by railway . . . '

There were innumerable pitfalls for young clergymen as he found out only too frequently and noted ruefully, as for instance:

'Thursday, May Morrow. I called on the Higginses, the new tenants at Clyro Court Farm. Mrs Higgins came into the drawing room with two other ladies, and if there is a mistake to be made I invariably make it so I accosted one of the ladies as Mrs Higgins and found afterwards that I was speaking to one of the Miss Bowens who always imagine that I know them so very well and who were therefore proportionately annoyed by the mistake . . .'

He was not always milk and water, however, as another entry soon afterwards indicated:

'Monday, 6 May. Got into an argument with Mr Latimer Jones about people's legal and moral rights over their property and he spoke in such an insolent and overbearing contemptuous way that my blood was up, and Mrs Bevan said afterwards she feared we should have fought.'

His emotions could be very readily aroused at times as he recorded, when reading to a veteran of the Peninsular Campaign:

'Wednesday, 8 May. I found the old soldier sitting in his house and read to him the remainder of that most touching story of Max Kromer and the Siege of Strasbourg. As I drew near the end of the book I became deeply affected and my voice was broken with emotion. My eyes filled with tears and I could scarcely see the page . . . and when I closed the book I was crying . . .'

His vicar, Mr Venables, wished him to stay on at Clyro as he noted, but he decided against it:

'Thursday, 23 May. This evening I had a letter from Mr Venables written yesterday (his birthday when he was 63) saying that he had decided not to resign the living of Clyro till the end of 1872 and offering me £160 a year to stay on. I decided to keep to my former plan and to leave Clyro at the beginning of August.'

In the event it was the end of August before he left, after rounds of present-givings and sad farewells from all his parishioners accompanied by numerous appeals to him to change his mind. He wrote:

'Sunday, September Day. My last day at Clyro. . . . In the afternoon I preached my farewell sermon . . . there were a good many people in Church. I don't know how I got through the service. It was the last time. My voice was broken and choked by sobs and tears, and I think the people in the Church were affected too. Richard Brooks in the choir was crying like a child.'

He returned home to act as curate to his father at Langley Burrell once again and a month later he chronicled:

'Monday, 14 October. . . . When I came down to breakfast I found on the table a letter from Mr Venables announcing the death of old Mr Thomas the Rector of Disserth, which took place last Friday. Mr Thomas's son immediately wrote to Mr Venables to beg that he would ask the Bishop to give him the living. This Mr Venables says that he at once declined to do and adds that he has written strongly to the Bishop . . . in my favour. . . . There is no house nor glebe and the living is saddled with Bettws Disserth, a chapelry where service must be performed every Sunday, 5 or 6 miles from Disserth Church. Mr Venables thinks notwithstanding that I should be unwise to decline the offer . . . should it be made to me. I hope the question may not arise. . . . Now I am settled here I do not want to leave my Father and this place and people to whom I am much attached, but yet I feel that I might throw away a fair chance of making myself a home and run the risk of finding myself adrift in the world, still a curate in middle age. . . . However, sufficient unto the day is the evil thereof . . .'

It had not taken him long to settle in happily at home once again and he did not seem to find his life confined in any way. Although there was little in the way of amusement, as an entry later in October indicated, it appeared to suit his simple tastes:

'Friday, 25 October. My Father is reading aloud to us in the evening that wild and powerful book *Lorna Doone*. Dear little Lorna.'

His views were sometimes surprisingly reactionary where his own affairs were concerned, as for example:

'Thursday, 8 May. . . . When I got home I heard that Anne Pugh, the housemaid . . . having been reproved for some negligence and sent with a note to Henry Cole's house, 4 minutes walk, had suddenly disappeared at 8.30 and had not been seen since. We supposed that she had bolted and gone home to Grittleton, 6 miles.

'Friday, 9 May. This morning early John Couzens was sent with the pony carriage to Grittleton to see what was become of Anne Pugh, the runaway servant. . . . At noon John returned driving Anne and her mother in the carriage to our great indignation and the poor pony's distress. I wouldn't have brought them in the carriage. I would have made them walk the whole way. A girl runs away from her place for no reason and the next morning has a carriage sent for her and drives back with her mother in state. This made me mad! I blamed John for bringing them in the carriage. John was much confused and trembled like a leaf. He said he didn't know what to do. . . . He hoped he should never be sent on such an errand again. The girl he declared ought to have been horsewhipped all the way back and sent to jail.'

Yet, though he might adhere to upper-class Victorian attitudes in some respects, Kilvert did not worry unduly about shocking the conventions as he noted in July:

'Thursday, 24 July. This morning Uncle Will, Dora and I drove to Seaton. . . . I had a bathe. A boy brought me to the machine door two towels as I thought, but when I came out of the water and began to use them I found that one of the rags he had given me was a pair of very short red and white striped drawers to cover up my nakedness. Un-accustomed to such things and customs I had in my ignorance bathed naked and set at nought the convention-alities of the place and scandalised the beach. However some little boys who were looking on at the rude naked man appeared to be much interested in the spectacle and the young ladies who were strolling near seemed to have no objection . . .'

He undoubtedly had a social conscience, even if it only worked with Victorian heaviness, stirring but slightly on occasions:

'Wednesday, 24 September. . . . As I walked before breakfast across the Common . . . I met Herriman the porter returning through the lovely morning from his night work at the station and I could not help thinking of the difference between my lot and his, and how much more enjoyment I have in my life than he has in his. . . . Herriman has only three days' holiday during the whole year, while to me every day is a holiday and enjoyment and delight. And for no desert of mine. Surely there will be compensation made for these things hereafter if not here.'

Despite their often ponderous and conventional attitudes, it is a mistake to imagine that the Victorians were easily misled about life, more especially the facts of life. Among many examples in Kilvert's diaries one in November 1873 will suffice:

'Thursday, 20 November. . . . We called at Francis Hall's. . . . They told us about Edith Headley's wedding. . . . Edward Humphries, the old pensioner, was there, aged 96. He married a young woman when he was 83 and had a son within the year. "Leastways his wife had," said Mrs Hall, with a cautious qualification of her former statement.'

Like so many other curates, Kilvert was not always a social success and was easily reduced to despondency, as in December of that year:

'Monday, 29 December. At 8.30 I went alone to a dance at the Ivy given by the Rookes. . . . Got home at 1.30. I felt like a fish out of water all the evening for I don't like round dances and don't understand the figures of the square dances so I spoil other people's fun. I don't think I shall go to a dance again.'

This resolution did not last long into 1874:

'Friday, 9 January. At 6 o'clock went to a dance at Norton Lodge with Dora. . . . It was a glorious evening. I never enjoyed anything more in my life . . .'

Langley Burrell apparently had its share of discreetly hidden sin, as he discovered in May:

'Saturday, May Morrow. Went to Peckingell. Found Austin a little better. He and his wife told me things about the parish which drew aside the veil from my eyes and showed me in what an atmosphere and abyss of wickedness we are living and how little many people are to be trusted whom we thought respectable and good . . .'

The vicarage at Langley Burrell, like so many others, was an old building, probably in a poor state of repair, and apparently infested with rats. He noted:

'Wednesday, 29 July. Last night the rats most provokingly carried off into their hole the contents of two dishes of apricots which had been gathered yesterday for our croquet party to-day and left on a shelf in the dining room closet.

'When I went to the Farm to drink my whey this morning I told them of our loss. Mrs Knight said that the rats went about overhead at night like race-horses, and Mary declared that the walls of their lower cheese room were lined with rats.

'The weather this afternoon was lovely, not too hot, a gentle air moving the silver birch, and bright gleams of sunshine threw beautiful shadows across the lawn, and the meadows. The lawn tennis was a successful diversion and afforded a good deal of amusement.

'About 30 people came, and we were disappointed of some 15.

'Nellie Andrews looked very pretty and charming in a pink dress.'

The following week a similar party turned out to be not quite so successful:

'Wednesday, 5 August. . . . We played croquet and lawn tennis in a drizzling rain . . .'

It was probably his own stern upbringing at his father's

hands, often the cause of a later interest in flagellation, which caused him to record the severe treatment of a young girl. It must, of course, be remembered that such attitudes to children were not at all uncommon in the Victorian period:

'Thursday, 6 August. I received this evening a . . . note from Susan Strange begging me to come and see her as soon as possible. . . . She was . . . troubled about her daughter Fanny, who grieves her sadly by frequently lying and stealing. I told her she must correct the girl in time. "I do flog her," she said . . .

'Saturday, 8 August. . . . I got a message . . . that little Fanny Strange had suddenly been taken ill and wanted to see me. I went immediately. The child was in bed upstairs. I sat down by her bed and took her hot little hand. She seemed very feverish but was quite sensible and appeared to be much softened and humbled. If so, the severe chastisement she has undergone may have had a happy effect and have broken her self-will and cured her of her faults. Her parents have very wisely not spared her nor the rod. She has during the last few weeks been repeatedly . . . flogged naked . . . At one time she seemed absolutely incorrigible. . . . The severest whippings her mother could inflict upon her bare flesh seemed to have no effect upon her. She was whipped . . . often twice or three times in the day and then when her father came home at night he got a stout switch, stripped the girl naked . . . and whipped her bare bottom and thighs again till they were covered with weals and the blood came. . . . But now happily the poor child has come to a better mind.'

In August of 1874 he was again passionately in love but Kathleen Mavourneen, as he called her, or Miss Kathleen Heanley, lived in Lincolnshire, which proved something of a handicap. Although this romance endured for some time it never reached the stage of approaching her father. Indeed from subsequent references it seems that Kilvert was intent on avoiding too much direct and ardent correspondence.

By October he was more concerned with the rats in the vicarage:

'Monday, 5 October. . . . The rats in my bedroom at the North-west corner of the house make a horrible noise at night. Sometimes they seem to be pulling down the walls. Sometimes they play bowls and skittles . . .'

Later in October there was a storm in a teacup over the dismissal of the chief singer by the Squire, Mr Ashe, who ruled the parish affairs with a rod of iron. Francis Kilvert was not disposed to accept his interference without a struggle:

'Wednesday, 28 October. This morning we held a family conclave and indignation meeting about the Church singing. At least we resolved that as Mr Ashe has practically dismissed George Jefferies from his post as leader of the singing and rendered it impossible . . . to go on upon the old footing, we must . . . have a harmonium or some instrument in the Church whether he likes it or not. We are prepared to give up the living and leave the place should we be obliged to do so rather than submit any longer to this tyranny. I don't think it will come to this. No such luck as to leave Langley. We should all be better and happier else-where, more independent and what is most important of all we should have more self-respect. For my own part I should for many reasons be glad and thankful to go. I don't know how it will end. I suppose I shall stay here as long as my Father lives, no longer . . .

'Thursday, 29 October. At 8.30 this morning we sent the harmonium to the Church. . . . Though a small instrument it quite filled the Church with sound. . . . How this inno-vation . . . will be received by the Squire no one can tell . . . we expect some violence of language at least . . .'

In the event everything went off quite well and the Squire made no comment at all, but attended church twice. Just the same he had the last word, as Kilvert recorded:

'Sunday, 8 November. . . . After morning service Dora went out to Mr Ashe in the churchyard and asked him to head the subscription list to buy a new harmonium. He said that neither he nor any of his household should give a farthing for he disapproved of any music in a church beside the human voice and he also apprehended a chronic difficulty in finding someone to play the instrument. I walked from church with dear Sarah Hicks to her house at the Pound.

'"Oh," she said earnestly, with indignant tears swelling in her beautiful large dark eyes, "oh, it's a comfort to know that there's a time coming when no one will be able to reign over us and when we shall be as good as those who are so high and proud over us now."

'Patience, dear Sarah, patience a little while longer. And then . . .'

His entry for his thirty-fifth birthday is revealing:

'Thursday, 3 December. My 35th birthday. May God give me grace that if I should be spared another year I may spend it better than the last.

'On my dressing table I found this morning a note from my dear Father enclosing a cheque for £5. My mother gave me Dorothy Wordsworth's *Journal*. Fanny and Dora had each had a picture framed and glazed for me. Katie with Doris's help had made a very pretty picture frame of paper.

'Toby gave me a stick of red sealing wax which to his great consternation was broken in three places, but which had been cleverly mended again.

'I had letters from Mother, Thersie, Teddy, Sallie Vaughan, Addie Heanley, Marion Vaughan, Mrs Venables, Mrs Cowper Coles, Mary Bevan, Emily Dew, Jane Dew and Alice Dew, Mrs Venables sent me Faber's Hymns and Mrs Cowper Coles gave me a little book which I hope and think will be of great use and help to me, *Holy Thoughts and Prayers* edited by Dr Hook.'

In April of the following year 1875 he noted that his old parish of Clyro was not faring well under its new vicar:

'Monday, 5 April. . . . At Hereford Station I fell in with

Higgins of the Court Farm, Clyro, who told me that poor dear old Clyro is all at sixes and sevens and the church and school nearly empty. He himself goes to Llowes Church. The new vicar (Prickard) seems to have been unwise in introducing several changes suddenly and so alienating and disturbing the people . . .'

Kilvert's account of a small incident in August again revealed his unconscious obsession with 'bare flesh'.

'Thursday, 12 August. I walked across to Kingston St. Michael to be present at the school feast.

'As we were swinging the children under the elms . . . a girl came up to me . . . for a swing. She was a perfect little beauty, with a plump rosy face, dark hair and lovely soft dark eyes . . . I lifted her onto the swing and away she went. But about the sixth flight the girl suddenly slipped off the swing feet foremost and still keeping hold of the ropes she hung from the swing helpless. Unfortunately . . . it instantly became apparent that she wore no drawers . . . a shout of laughter ran through the crowd as the girl's plump person was seen naked hanging from the swing. . . . I believe it was partly my fault . . . I suppose I set her down with her clothes rumpled up and her bare flesh (poor child) upon the board and as her flesh was plump and smooth and in excellent whipping condition and the board slippery, they managed to part company, with this result . . .'

Francis Kilvert obviously had considerable charm, attracting both young and old of all classes. Apart from his evidently happy, pleasing personality this was probably due in part to his mellifluous voice, to judge by his father's comment on his preaching in 1876:

'Sunday, 19 March. . . . As we came in at the orchard door together after the morning service my dear Father said "As you were preaching there came back upon my ear an echo of the tones of the sweetest human voice I ever heard, the voice of John Henry Newman. No voice but yours ever reminded me of him.'

Soon afterwards a clandestine poetical romance he had been conducting with a Miss Ettie Meredith Brown, still not out of school, was nipped in the bud:

'Thursday, 20 April. I received a long and sad sweet loving letter from my darling Ettie, a tender beautiful letter of farewell, the last she will ever be able to write to me. With it came enclosed a kind friendly little note from young Mrs Meredith Brown . . . saying she is afraid Ettie and I must hold no further communication by letter or poetry or in any other way. . . . She is right and I have been, alas, very, very wrong . . . Ettie my own only lost love . . . my own dear little girl.'

In June 1876 came what seemed to be his opportunity at last:

'Trinity Sunday, 11 June. . . . This morning came a letter from the Bishop of St. David's offering me the Vicarage of St. Harmon's. I wrote and accepted it. Then it has come at last and I must leave my dear old home and parish and say goodbye to Langley and all my dear kind friends there. It will be a hard and bitter wrench and a sorrowful, a very sorrowful parting. It seems dreadful to leave my Father alone at his age and with his infirmities to contend with the worries and anxieties of the parish and at the tender mercies of a curate. I hope I have not acted selfishly in leaving him. But at my age I feel I cannot throw away a chance in life and our tenure of this living is a very precarious one. It is "the warm nest on the rotten bough." I have not sought this or any other preferment. Indeed I have rather shrunk from it. And as it has come to me without my wish . . . it seems as if the Finger of God were in it . . .'

The record of Francis Kilvert's life at St. Harmon's is unfortunately missing, but his diaries resumed again in December 1877, by which time he had become vicar of Bredwardine in Herefordshire and his sister Dora was keeping house for him. Here he noted that his father was the first to preach ' in the year of grace 1878' in Bredwardine church. Still hale and hearty, although well into his seventies, Robert Kilvert was to outlive his son.

There is a pleasant description of a tithe dinner in 1878 presided over by a Francis Kilvert already developing in stature and authority, in a living worth £375 per annum.

'Tuesday, 5 February. To-day was the Tithe audit and tithe dinner to the farmers, both held at the Vicarage. About fifty tithe payers came, most of them very small holders, some paying as little as 9d. As soon as they had paid their tithe to Mr Haywood in the front hall they retired into the back hall and regaled themselves with bread, cheese and beer, some of them eating and drinking the value of the tithe they had paid. The tithe paying began at 3 p.m. and the stream went on till six. At 7 I sat down to dinner with the farmers. Haywood took the foot of the table. His son sat on my left and Price of Bodcote on my right hand . . .

'The Pen Pistyll turkey boiled looked very noble when it came to table. George Davies of Benfield was so impressed with the size of the bird he declared it must be a "three year old" and he did not hear the last of this all evening. At the foot of the table there was roast beef, and at the sides jugged hare and beafsteak pie, preceded by pea soup, and in due course followed by plum pudding, apple tart, mince pies and blancmange, cheese and dessert. It was a very nice dinner thanks to Dora and I think they all liked it and enjoyed themselves. After dinner Haywood proposed my health very kindly and I made a little speech. We broke up at 10.30 . . .'

In June his cough was worse and his health proving troublesome. A significant series of entries ran:

'Thursday, 20 June. In the morning I weeded the raspberry bed in the lower garden. Afternoon walked to a garden party at Eardisley Vicarage. A very pleasant evening. Palmer took me aside as soon as I came in and offered me from Canon Walsham How the permanent Chaplaincy at Cannes. He thought it might perhaps be desirable to accept it on account of my health.

'Saturday, 22 June. A fine summer's day. Very hot . . . called on Miss Cornewell who has lately come back from Cannes to ask her for information about the place. She was very kind and told me much. She said she thought the Chaplaincy must be a very delightful position. Mr Giles came in to see one of the servants. I asked if I ought to go to Cannes on account of my health. He said "Go by all means. It is the very place. It may prolong your life for some years."'

Finally, after some indecision, there came the firm entry:

'Thursday, 27 June. . . . Wrote to Palmer and Walsham How to decline the Cannes Chaplaincy . . .'

He had just over a year left to live and the diary ends abruptly in the March of 1879. Only the bare facts of his marriage on the 20th of August and his death some five weeks later are known, but they are unimportant. Although he died the vicar of Bredwardine it was no doubt as the curate of Clyro and Langley Burrell that his friends remembered him best. It was thus that he had spent the greatest part of his life and it is as a curate of infinite promise that he lives on in his diaries.

# Select Bibliography

Clegg, The Rev. James (1679-1755). *Extracts from the Diary . . . of the Rev. James Clegg*, ed. Henry Kirk (London, 1899).

Cole, The Rev. William (1714-1782). *The Blecheley Diary of Rev. William Cole*, ed. F.G. Stokes (London, 1931).

Jones, The Rev. William (1755-1821). *The Diary of the Reverend William Jones*, ed. O.F. Christie (London, 1929).

Josselin, The Rev. Ralph (1616-1683). *The Diary of the Rev. Ralph Josselin*, ed. E. Hockcliffe (Royal Hist. Soc., London, 1908).

Kilvert, The Rev. Francis (1840-1879). *Kilvert's Diary*, ed. William Plomer, 3 vols. (London, 1938-1940).

Newton, The Rev. Benjamin (1762-1830). *The Diary of Benjamin Newton*, ed. C.P. Fendall and E.A. Crutchley (Cambridge, 1933).

Ridpath, The Rev. George (1717-1772). *Diary of George Ridpath*, ed. Sir J.B. Paul (Scottish Hist. Soc., Edinburgh, 1922).

Sage, The Rev. Donald (1789-1869). *Memorabilia Domestica; or Parish Life in the North of Scotland*, ed. D.F. Sage (Wick, 1889).

Skinner, The Rev. John (1772-1839). *Journal of a Somerset Rector*, ed. H. Coombs and A.N. Bax (London, 1930).

Stevenson, The Rev. Seth Ellis (1724-1783). Clerical diary, 1752-1755. MS Wigan Central Public Library.

Turnbull, The Rev. John (1657-1744). Religious diary, 1686-1704. *Miscellany of Scottish Hist. Soc.*, I (Edinburgh, 1893).

Woodforde, The Rev. James (1740-1803). *The Diary of a Country Parson*, ed. John Beresford, 5 vols. (London, 1924-1931).

# Further Reading

Addison, William. *English Country Parson*, Dent, 1947.

Atkinson, J.C. *Forty Years in a Moorland Parish*, MacMillan, 1907.

Baring-Gould, Sabine. *The Vicar of Morwenstow: 1896.*

Bax, B. Anthony. *The English Parsonage*, John Murray, 1964.

Baxter, Richard. *Reliquiae Baxterianae*, 1696.

Bonar, The Rev. Andrew Alexander (1810-1892). *Diary and Letters of Rev. Andrew Bonar*, ed. M. Bonar (London, 1894).

Brown, C.K.F. *A story of the English Clergy 1800-1900*, 1953.

Bullett, Gerald. *Sydney Smith*, Michael Joseph, 1951.

Byles, C.E. *Life & Letters of R.S. Hawker*, Lane, 1905.

Craik, The Rev. Henry. *Passages from the Diary and Letters of Henry Craik of Bristol*, (Bristol, 1866).

Cullum, The Rev. Thomas Gery. Travel diaries, 1767-1832. 67 journals. MS Bury St. Edmunds Public Library.

Davies, E.W.L. *Memoir of the Rev. John Russell 1883.*

Ditchfield, P.H. *The Old Time Parson*, Methuen, 1908.

Ellman, E.B. *Recollections of a Sussex Parson*, Cambridge, 1912.

Hannington, The Rt. Rev. James (1847-1885). *James Hannington*, Edwin C. Dawson (London, 1887); *The Last Journals of James Hannington*, ed. E.C. Dawson (London, 1888).

Hart, A. Tindal. *Country Priest*, Phoenix, 1959.

Moorman, J.R.H. *A History of the Church of England*, 1953.

Newcombe, The Rev. Henry Justinian. *The Lunatic or English Clergymen and Scotch Doctors: An Autobiography* (London, 1861).

Stoner, The Rev. David (1794-1826). *Memoirs of Rev. David Stoner*, (London, 1828).

White, The Rev. Gilbert (1720-1793). *Journals of Gilbert White*, ed. W. Johnson, (London, 1931).

Wood, The Rev. J. (1797-1869). *The Life of the Rev. J. Wood*, Henry W. Williams, (London, 1871).